LONGDOGS BY DAY

LONGDOGS BY DAY

E. G. Walsh

THE BOYDELL PRESS

First published 1990 by The Boydell Press, Woodbridge

The Boydell Press is an imprint of Boydell & Brewer Ltd
PO Box 9, Woodbridge, Suffolk IP12 3DF

ISBN 0 85115 266 X

British Library Cataloguing in Publication Data
Walsh, E. C. (Edward Geoffrey), *1917–*
  Longdogs by day.
  1. Hounds for coursing
  I. Title
  636.7′53
ISBN 0-85115-266-X

This publication is produced on acid-free paper

Printed in Great Britain by St Edmundsbury Press, Bury St Edmunds, Suffolk

CONTENTS

ILLUSTRATIONS

20. A distinguished visitor, Mr M.A.Bhutto, one-time Finance Minister of Pakistan and Governor of Sind Province, who hunts wild boar in Pakistan with longdogs
21. 1985; Phil Lloyd, judge, Small Reserve Champion Mr Colling-Fletcher's *Dolly*, Small Champion Mr Lumb's *Jed* and John Bromiley, judge
22. 1985; Tom Davies, judge, Large Reserve Champion Mrs Newbury's *Gemma*, Large Champion Mr Squires' *Miller*, Dick Finch, judge
23. 1985; Mrs Walwyn with the Reserve Supreme Champion, Mr Lumb's *Jed*
24. 1985; Mrs Walwyn with the Supreme Champion, Mr Squires' *Miller*, ably handled by Karen Hemes whilst his owner was busy combining
25. Faces at Shows
    a. Penny Lowis
    b. Leesa Sandys-Lumsdaine
    c. Michael Forsyth-Forrest
    d. George Smith
26. Faces at Shows
    a. Elspeth Mackie
    b. Tony Mills
    c. Bert Gripton
    d. Roy Ware
27. Faces at Shows
    a. 'Ginger' French
    b. Sue Sowerby
    c. Phil Lloyd
    d. Maurice Salkeld
28. Faces at Shows
    a. Caroline Gentry
    b. Brian Peters
    c. Peter Ince
    d. David Gaydon
29. Faces at Shows
    a. Eddie Jones
    b. Tony Diprose
    c. Dave McKnie
    d. John Bromiley
30. Faces at Shows
    a. Janis Willingale
    b. Tony Palmer
    c. Alf Graham
    d. David Hancock
31. Faces at Shows
    a. Delyth Jones
    b. Vic Gardner, whose magazine, *Shooting News*, sponsored the SNUK Championship Show at Towcester

c. Dave Todd

d. Lucy Clegg

OTHER SHOW ACTIVITIES

RACING

SPEED JUMPING

HIGH JUMPING

SHOW JUMPING

OBEDIENCE

PART II. LONGDOGS AT WORK: COURSING

PRIVATE COURSING AS IT WAS

COURSING: THE PURE BREEDS

GREYHOUNDS

231. The meeting can be formal, with a Slipper and a Judge (on foot)
232. Lurchers are usually held in single slips
233. Walking up a hare
234. Slipping on rape
235. A less formal meeting will dispense with the slipper and owners will slip their own dogs, the two to run walking in front of the line
236. At an even less formal meeting where dogs are slipped from where they walk the line can be half a mile long
237. The line needs to be shorter on cover, such as rape, or hares will be walked over
238. Lurchers are not as fast as greyhounds but from their cross-breeding can have tremendous stamina
239. A fawn and a brindle turn the hare from a wood
240. A hare off rape making for the wood and safety
241. Lurchers coursing
242. Lurchers coursing
243. A solo course
244. This hare beat the two dogs by spinning round on its hind legs every time they snatched at it until it got to the wood in safety
245. Two rough dogs settle down for a long run
246. As in public coursing, a third dog does sometimes join in
247. *Len* carrying the hare
248. *Badger* very tired

INTRODUCTION

This is a picture book of Longdogs; cross-bred at play at lurcher shows and pure-bred and cross-bred at work by day, coursing.

When I was writing a book about lurchers in 1975–76 I used the title *'Lurchers and Longdogs'*. It had a nice alliterative ring about it and it described the contents but before the book went to print I was asked what the difference was. Having been used to the word since childhood to describe any dog of greyhound type with a long tail (long head, long legs, long body etc.), or perhaps something or someone that moved like one – 'he ran up the street like a longdog', – I had not thought that a definition was necessary. However it appeared that I would have to do something about it and I wrote the description which appears on page xiii of *Lurchers and Longdogs*: 'any longtail but in this context the offspring of a coursing dog and a coursing dog'. I thought no more about it but over the ensuing years I have seen what I had scribbled on the back of an envelope at a moment's notice taken all too seriously; to the extent that I recently read a solemn pronouncement on the number of eighths part collie that would turn a longdog into a lurcher, or some such nonsense.

My original title, *Lurchers and Longdogs*, seems to be used now by all and sundry, including some magazine writers as a title for their articles, but all enquirers have to do is to look in a dictionary. The O.E.D. duly gives 'longdog: *dialect*, a greyhound'. So, to define it again (and this time I am not pulling anyone's leg), a *longdog* is a dog that is long everywhere: long head, long neck, long back, long legs and long tail, be it pure-bred or cross-bred. It is tempting to carry on and say that a longdog can be a lurcher but a lurcher is not necessarily a longdog but what is the point, dear Reader? Someone is bound to take it seriously and make further solemn pronouncements on the subject!

Part I of the book is a look at lurcher shows from the beginning in 1971 to 1988 but it is, inevitably, a restricted look. With lurcher shows taking place throughout the Summer from one end of the country to the other, and as many as ten and more shows on a Sunday in July and August, no one person can attend them all and I have not, for various reasons, commented on every one of the many shows that I have been to. Since my records are not complete nor, I fear, absolutely accurate I may have given the wrong names to some dogs and people, in which case I apologise to them. As well as descriptions of shows I give my methods of judging lurchers and some advice for those who may be press-ganged into doing ring steward. I have included some comments on 'other activities', racing, jumping, etc., as I know that many lurcher owners enjoy them. I am still doubtful in my own mind about obedience for lurchers

1

beyond a certain point but those who do train their dogs to a high state of obedience have my unstinted admiration.

Part II is about coursing, both private and public. I have tried to illustrate some of the Rules of the National Coursing Club which govern what actually happens at a coursing meeting; the Rules, particularly those dealing with judging a course, are complicated to someone who has not seen coursing before and I hope that illustrations may help to make some of them clearer. My comments on lurcher coursing are, of course, my own and I know that some of them will not please everyone.

Nearly all the photographs are my own and the faults in them are mine. Many of the early show photos were taken in colour and I have had to reprint in black and white from colour negatives or to copy; not difficult but it can add denseness to a print. Where the photo was taken by someone else it is attributed alongside and my thanks to Peter Goulding, Phil Lloyd and Ralph Jeffries for permission to use their property. My thanks also to Charles Blanning, Secretary of the National Coursing Club, for permission to reproduce some of the N.C.C. Rules and to the Editor of *Shooting Times* for permission to reprint extracts of text and photos which had previously appeared in that magazine.

Whilst I have tried to include photos from the shows I mention in the text it has not always been possible. Looking back, I find that my photo coverage has been uneven, with many photos from some shows and few, or none, from others. It has partly depended on whether I was judging or not; when judging I have always tried to photograph at least the Champion and Reserve if not some of the class winners, but coverage of the show as a whole has usually been nil; one is too busy in the ring. I have included some prints from my 'Rogues Gallery', if they will excuse the term, of people who are, or were seen at lurcher shows either as organisers, exhibitors or judges; sadly, some are no longer with us but most of them are, I trust and hope, fit and well. The list is not, in any way at all, comprehensive. I have also included some photos of 'dogs from shows'. One or two are already pictured at the shows concerned, others are from the many photos I have taken of dogs that caught my eye. They have in common the fact that they all at least won classes and many won championships or reserves so others (including me, for I have judged the majority of them) besides the owners liked the look of them. Some I have seen working and others' work I know of by repute. Where I can trace the names I have given them; for the others I have given the place and date of the photo. I leave it to the reader to decide whether he agrees with the judges' decisions or not. I hope that owners will recognise their own dogs.

Professional photographers will deride my offerings of coursing photos but my experience has been that it is often more a matter of luck than good judgement; photographing steeplechasing is easy compared to coursing. One is trying to take pictures of a hare and two dogs, travelling at up to 35mph at distances varying – and varying very quickly – from close-up to 'out of sight over the hill'. The hare stands no more than twelve inches high and in winter is the same colour as stubble or old, dry grass. This also applies to whippets;

the dogs at a distance look not much bigger than the hare and fawn whippets will also disappear in stubble. Greyhounds are of course easier and salukis easier still; the latter are showy dogs and they do not gallop or turn quite so fast as the other two. All this with a 300 or 400mm lens with a depth of focus of about two dogs' lengths! Stand on this side of the running ground at a driven meeting and the hares from the beat go up the other side and turn away into the far hedge; stand on the other side and either the sun, rain or sleet is in one's face and onto the face of the camera lens. At a walked meeting one often has to anticipate fields ahead, carrying up to 20lbs of equipment. Add the fact that by 2pm on a December or January afternoon the light has usually 'gone' for normal photographic purposes and I am often amazed that there is anything to show on the strips of negatives when I have developed them.

Still, it is is a wonderful sport; long may it still last despite developers and environmentalists. As always, my thanks to the Secretaries of the Alresford, Cotswold, Huntingdon, Newmarket and South of England and the Oxford Coursing Clubs for permission to take photographs at their meetings over many years.

Ted Walsh
June 1989

PART I
LONGDOGS AT PLAY

Chapter 1

LURCHER SHOWS

The first Dog Show took place at Newcastle in 1859, followed by another at Birmingham the same year. Although Charles Cruft had been running shows for Spratts, the dog biscuit makers, for some years, he announced the First Great Terrier Show in 1886 which in turn became the present day 'Crufts'. The first Hound Show of any size took place at Redcar, also in 1859 and Peterborough, the premier Hound Show, was started in 1879. Compared to what might be called the 'legitimate' shows, lurcher shows are very much newcomers, starting in 1971 at Lambourn, in Berkshire.

Lambourn having begun it all, lurcher shows sprang up almost overnight and they fell into four main classes: pure lurcher shows, shows run by Hunts or Hunt Supporters Clubs, shows held at Country Fairs and shows run by lurcher clubs, lurcher/terrier clubs and terrier clubs.

The pure lurcher shows were good and enjoyable shows. They were run by lurcher people for lurcher people and, so far as I know, all contributed sums of money, often surprisingly large, to various charities. I use the past tense because most of these shows are now no more. They finished because in almost every case the organisers were no longer prepared to carry on under extreme aggravation from a minority of the people attending their shows and they saw no future or point in running them.

In the second category, I have counted some 74 packs of hounds whose Hunt Supporters Clubs have run or still run lurcher shows. Some were and are good, some fair and some indifferent, depending on whether the organisers were lurcher people or not. Maintaining a pack of hounds is an expensive business, varying of course on the position and 'smartness' of the pack. Four days a week in Leicestershire is a very different matter from a 'provincial' farmers pack who may manage on less than a quarter of the Leicestershire income, but wherever they are, whether they be foxhounds or beagles, they cost more than the subscriptions amount to and the extra must be found somewhere. 'Somewhere' includes raffles, dances, 'caps', open days, fun days, horse shows, terrier shows etc, etc, and when lurcher shows started many Hunt Supporters Clubs saw them as money raisers. Herein lies an anomaly for, while lurcher people are happy to attend Hunt shows and Hunts are ready to take their money off them, let a lurcher man ask a hunting landowner or hunting farmer for permission to look for a hare or rabbit with his dog and he was, and is, at the best told to remove himself quickly and at the worst shown the business end of a shot gun. Some years ago the Master of Foxhounds Association sent a letter to Hunts advising them not to run lurcher shows; the following year's show list showed an increase of 33 per cent in Hunt Supporters Club run shows. One is tempted to ask whether the dog wagged the tail or the tail the dog, but of course Supporters Clubs are largely answerable to themselves.

Of the Hunt shows, the three best are no longer run: Whaddon Chase, Heythrop and Cottesmore. Of the shows still being run, some attract entries as low as one or two per class and the largest class that can usually be expected is under 20. When I was writing regularly about lurchers in *Shooting Times* I tried to encourage adjacent Hunts to liaise in order not to run shows on the same day, or to amalgamate and thus share the overheads. Being individualists there were no amalgamations and some wonder why their takings hardly cover expenses.

The third category, lurcher shows held at Country Fairs, are a mixed blessing. Some are quite good, some not worth walking round the corner to attend. One of the problems is the car park fee. The organisers want to make money; they lay on everything they can possibly cram into the ground, advertise it as a wonderful day out for the family and charge attendance fees accordingly. The lurcher man who merely wants to show his dog and is not in the least interested in clay pigeon shooting, parades of vintage cars, sheep dog demonstrations, bagpipe blowing, (I once judged at Holkham with seven pipe bands practising within splitting earshot of the ring), sidesaddle riding and morris dancing, objects to paying £4 or even £5 a head to get his car into a car park half a mile from the lurcher ring. A second snag to such shows is the fact that not being lurcher people themselves the organisers fail to get judges and other officials of sufficient calibre – and sometimes of no calibre at all. Where lurcher people are asked to run the lurcher part of a Country Fair they are often not given anything like enough room; here I instance Lowther where Maurice Salkeld had to manage for several years with a ring hardly big enough for terriers. When the lurcher ring was moved up the hillside above the main car park the Lowther Lurcher Show came into its own as one of the best in the country. Sadly, due to local prejudice it is no more.

In the fourth category come the shows run by lurcher clubs, lurcher/terrier clubs and terrier clubs. They are usually well worth attending since they are – usually – run by knowledgeable people but by no means always. I have been to some really terrible shows run by people who should have known better: rings far too small, nothing like enough parking for cars, not enough schedules, judges apparently judging for the first time. Still, one hopes that they profit from their mistakes and get it right next time.

So much for a brief look at seventeen years of lurcher shows.

Lurcher shows take place on Sundays – a few are held on Saturdays but the attendance is almost always poor – and because there are only so many Sundays between Spring and Autumn there may be several weekends in mid and late summer with up to eight or more shows on one day. In addition some shows are only advertised locally or even advertised at the last minute. One person cannot attend every lurcher show (what a terrible thought) so I can only comment on lurchers shows which I have seen.

The first organised show took place at Lambourn in 1971. By 1978 some 25 shows were advertised in *Shooting Times,* this figure rising to 80 in 1982, 101 in 1984, 140 in 1985 and 150 in 1986, the last year that I did the list. To these numbers one can probably add another 25 per cent for those shows that did not take advantage of free advertising or who did not complete and send in their proformas in time and sent in details later under 'forthcoming attractions'. The 1989 Terrier Show list contains 120 lurcher shows; again, this will not be the final number as some organisers did not send in their details by the publication date. I start with some of the shows that are no more and, to begin at the beginning, the first and the greatest of them all was Lambourn.

The Lambourn Lurcher Show was the show that started it all in 1971 and which grew to a size, and notoriety, that no other show has approached or will approach, for better or for worse. Lambourn, in Berkshire, is the largest racehorse training centre outside Newmarket. Many of its inhabitants are also coursing enthusiasts and they tend to keep running and hunting dogs, lurchers and terriers, greyhounds and whippets. I once asked the late Leesa Sandys-Lumsdaine, the artist and lurcher and greyhound breeder, how the show started. She wrote, 'It all started in a most amateur way. We used to have mixed dog gatherings with picnics and racing after a dummy hare – staggered starts, handicaps and races for all sorts and sizes. After one particularly good lunch we suddenly thought we would run a lurcher show on the lines of the numerous terrier shows and, in a mad rush, got everything organised, sent out schedules to everyone we thought might be interested and put an ad in the sporting papers. The week leading up to the show was hectic as we did all the refreshments ourselves and put up an ancient, patched marquee with hilarious help from Fred Winter's lads. John Mason and John Pattinson judged and we had about 100 entries in the six classes. It was great fun and although we didn't have any sponsors we were pleased to make £60 for the Injured Jockeys Fund; and when the show appeared on TV news we had literally hundreds of indignant enquiries from lurcher people who were furious at having missed it'.

The 'ancient tent' had been put up in the field in front of Captain and Mrs Lowis' house at Upper Lambourn, Mrs Penny Lowis, as she then was, being one of the organisers; Fred Winter ran the racing for all sorts and conditions of dogs and many others from the racing community helped in many ways. Over the next three years Penny Lowis watched the show growing; she, and some of the others, felt like the Sorcerer's Apprentice, unable to control the gathering storm. The fun afternoon they had started was getting out of hand. The show ran at the Lowis' house until 1974 and then stopped. Apart from other reasons the ground was no longer available. I have not got names for the Champions in

1972 and 1974 but the first Champion of all was Mrs Dibble's *Grey* in 1971 and Ian Balding's *Bertie* got the title in 1973. On a personal note, my *Tarn* won the smooth bitch class as a puppy in 1974 and was second to George Smith's *Tip* in a large puppy class, large for those early days but perhaps a third of the entries of later years.

There was no show in 1975 but a new Committee was formed under the chairmanship of Peter Tabor and in 1976 the Lambourn Lurcher Show re-started at Seven Barrows, in front of Peter Walwyn's training stables. There was the usual division for dogs at over and under 22 inches, with nine classes for each height: Rough Dog, Smooth Dog, Rough Bitch, Smooth Bitch, Puppy (under one year old), Veteran (over 10 years old), Pairs, Progeny (4 or more) and the Large and Small Championships open to winners of the classes down to veteran. I have no note of entry numbers but I was judging the large ring that year with Roddy Armytage, the trainer, and I think our entries were about 25 in a class; the under-22-inch judges were Leesa Sandys-Lumsdaine and James Daly, MFH. The Supreme Champion was Michael Goodman's *Peggy*, a large, dark grey, rough-coated bitch.

In 1977 the judges were James Daly and Mary Browning, the well-known artist, for the large ring and John McCririck – who needs no introduction for Channel 4 racing fans – and Mrs Ransom, greyhound breeder and one-time MFH, for the under-22s ring. Entries in the four main classes were 178 large and 70 small and the overall entries, including racing, obedience and jumping, totalled 800. The Supreme Champion was Ian Balding's *Bertie*, Champion for the second time.

For 1978 there were three rings, one for large rough, one for large smooth and one for under-22 inches. I judged the large rough ring with an entry of 186 dogs, bitches and puppies; Mick White, lurcher and terrier man, judged the smooth ring with an total of 108 and Mrs 'George' Barclay judged the under-22 ring with a total of 134. Overall entries were 906 and the Supreme Champion was Mr Hobden's *Kizzie*, again a nice, dark rough-coated bitch. Mrs 'Bumble' Upton was now the Show Secretary and carried on that arduous task until the end in 1985.

In 1979 there were four rings, large rough, large smooth, small rough and small smooth, the judges being Mrs Lilah Shennan, then Chairman of the National Coursing Club, (assisted by her nephew, James Daly), Mrs 'George' Barclay, Aubrey Fryer, lurcher breeder and Mr and Mrs Delahooke, of the Adstock Stud. I have not got notes of all the entries but there were 91 large rough dogs, 92 large rough bitches and 70 large smooth bitches; the total entries were 1,240. The Supreme Champion was Rob Matt's *Pip*, bred by George Smith. I see from *Shooting Times* that I commented on the fact that the rings were too small, despite the amount of ground available.

For 1980, despite advice to the contrary, the Committee appointed two judges for each ring; they were John Corkhill and Michael Lyne (the artist and saluki breeder), Brian Plummer and Maurice Salkeld, Mrs Tarn Riley and Brandon Cadbury and Michael Forsyth-Forrest (greyhound trainer) and Dave

Todd. The Supreme Champion was Mrs Sykes' *Sandy*. I have no figures for entries this year.

In 1981 the judges were myself for the large rough ring (I had refused to judge in pairs), Leesa Sandys-Lumsdaine and Michael Morley, the trainer, for large smooth, Moses Aaron Smith and Martin Knowelden for small rough and Mrs Flavia Cadbury and Dermot Kelly, MFH, for small smooth. I have no note of overall entries but I had about 300, or maybe more, in three classes and there were about 1,300 cars. It was a blisteringly hot day and I felt sorry for the rough dogs. With the numbers to be judged we did not reach the final championship until after 4pm by which time three of the judges had gone to lunch and not returned. So four of us agreed without much argument on Mrs Rose Lloyd's *Lucy* as the Supreme Champion. There were some very nice dogs at Lambourn that year and I particularly remember Major Scott's *Rollo*, a powerful red fawn dog; I think he was beaten by *Lucy* because he looked more like a greyhound while she was, and still is, obviously lurcher. The small Champion and Reserve Supreme was Roy Cox's *Sam*.

When the Show had been at Upper Lambourn the ground was surrounded by hedges and the railings in front of the Lowis' house but at Seven Barrows the ground was on the lower slopes of Berkshire downland, seemingly unlimited room, which, with hindsight, was its undoing. The crowd increased each year and included many travellers – who had attended in smaller numbers from the start – and some hooligans in search of trouble. The sight of those open downs with the promise of sport and hares was too enticing and they took advantage of it. Gangs of gypsies were arriving a week before the Show and spending the intervening days poaching, threatening anyone who tried to stop them. The crunch came in 1982.

Once again there were eight judges for the four rings. The overall entries totalled 1,400 and once again the rings were too small. After a long discussion the rule-of-thumb – 'rough beats smooth, large beats small' – prevailed and the eight judges gave the Supreme Championship to Mick Cawley's *Queenie*, a bitch he had rescued from a tinker's encampment, tied to a tent and so weak that he had to carry her to his car. She was, and is, a nice bitch and at Lambourn she showed no signs of her bad treatment. I mean no disrespect to *Queenie* or to the individual judges but I was reminded of the saying that 'A camel is a horse designed by a committee'. Three or even four people can usually come to a reasonable conclusion but the sight of eight judges arguing over the final line-up did not inspire confidence.

The crowd in 1982 was bigger than ever and whilst the final judging was taking place for the championship the voice of Richard Pitman, the commentator, was heard imploring the police to go to the beer tent; a bare-fist fight was taking place between two enormous travellers. It was rumoured that the police had wisely switched off their pocket telephones and the fight stopped by mutual consent after two rounds. Having been watching the judging I did not arrive at the 'fight' ringside until the contestants were hurrying off, mopping up the blood, and the crowd was dispersing. That night one of the Lambourn pubs was

11

broken up. The damage was inevitably blamed on lurcher people and, indeed, it was they who had done most of the breaking but several weeks later I was told a different story. It was to the effect that a local farmer had come into the bar somewhat the worse for drink and loudly blamed lurchers for killing some of his sheep. According to my informants – locals and not lurcher people – the killing had been done by two local unsupervised Labradors, not lurchers, and the lurcher men in the pub were perhaps within their rights, as they saw it, in beating up the farmer. But too much damage had been done over the years, culminating in the prize-fight. The Lambourn Show Committee and Lambourn village had had enough and both said 'No more'.

In answer to many appeals and against their better judgement the Lambourn Committee, now under the Chairmanship of Peter Walwyn who had hosted the show so generously and long-sufferingly at Seven Barrows, and still with Mrs Upton as Secretary, bravely re-started the show at Newbury Racecourse: Lambourn Mark III. The fact that it was no longer at Lambourn kept many away who would otherwise have attended and there were many complaints about having to park in the car park behind an eight foot wall and not in sight of the rings which were between the stands and the racecourse rails. Dog stealing has been and still is a constant threat at lurcher shows.

This year the Committee sensibly appointed only one judge per ring; they were James Daly, MFH, George Smith from Worcester, Carl Banner from Northampton and John Hunt from Dorset. With entries some 40 per cent down on the last Seven Barrows Show judging finished earlier than one had been used to for 'Lambourn', the Supreme Champion being Mr Watson's *Havoc* with Mr Tambling's *Jody*, a daughter of Roy Ware's redoubtable dog *Shep*, the Small Champion and Supreme Reserve Champion.

Finally to 1985, though at the time of the Show we did not know that it was the last. Again there were four judges, one per ring and again they were all lurcher men. They were Dick Finch from Northamptonshire, Thomas Morgan Davies from Wales, John Bromiley, then from Sussex, and Phil Lloyd from Hayling Island. The entries were possibly a little up on 1984 though I have not got exact figures now. The last and final Supreme Lambourn Champion was Peter Squires' *Miller*, bred by the late Sue Sowerby and ably handled by Karen Hemes, Miller's owner being busy combining at St Neots. The Small Champion and overall Reserve was Mr Lumb's *Jed*, a very strong whippet-type lurcher.

And so ended Lambourn. The entries did not justify the cost of using Newbury Racecourse and the Committee had had enough. Those who showed lurchers owed a great debt to Peter Walwyn for keeping the Show going for so long.

So, on, in less detail, to other shows.

It is probably invidious to rank lurcher shows so what I say in such matters is my opinion alone; others will, no doubt, disagree and that is their privilege. *In my opinion*, two shows ranked equal next to Lambourn – ranked because both are no more. One was the Whaddon Chase and the other was Lowther. Since the Whaddon ran for longer than Lowther I take that one first.

This show was started by the Whaddon Chase Hunt Supporters Association, 'The Whaddon Chasers', in 1977 at Merrymead Farm, near Bletchley, the property then of Dorian Williams, MFH. The show, for lurchers and terriers, was a success from the start. In 1978 Comdr David Dalton took over as Secretary, the show expanding as the Whaddon Chase Country Fair and Lurcher and Terrier Show; clay pigeon shooting was available for those who wished to shoot and there was inter-pub tug-of-war. The 'Whaddon' quickly became firmly established on the second Sunday in June, the lurcher part of the show owing much of its success to the enthusiasm and knowledge of the late Sue Sowerby who owned, bred and above all worked a most successful line of large lurchers, including the last Lambourn Champion of all, Mr Squires' *Miller*. The show was held in an enclosed field, both at Mursley and at Stoke Hammond where it moved for the final year and as the bar was not too close to the rings or to the car parks there was never any real trouble at Whaddon and entries were always good and high class. A feature of Whaddon was the fact that instead of one Supreme Champion there were Championships for the Large Rough, Large Smooth, Small Lurchers and the Puppies. This meant that judges did not have to choose between large and small, always an invidious job as they are different dogs for different purposes. The rings were always big enough for the largest classes, the timing was immaculate and Whaddon was a show at which it was a pleasure to judge.

Only in one year did the Whaddon not come quite up to its high standard and that was in 1983 when June was so wet that the Committee realised early enough that cars would have to be towed both into and out of the ground; the show was postponed to the second Sunday in September. It so happened that on that Saturday night came the first really hard rain since mid-summer and the rain, combined with a bitingly cold wind and the established Welsh Lurcher Club Show on the same date meant that entries were down by 20 per cent and car park takings, on which shows depend for the jam on the bread, down by nearly 50 per cent. Nevertheless there was no lack of quality in the dogs that did come to Mursley and with fewer public it was easier to walk round the rings. Amongst others was Mrs Cawley's *Gyp*, daughter of the 1982 Lambourn winner *Queenie*, who won the Puppy Championship and Tony Mills came with that great dog *Biff*, one of the best movers I have seen amongst lurchers.

In 1985 the last Whaddon was held at Mursley, with a Press Release no less, stating that it was the biggest Lurcher and Terrier Show in the country. There were larger terrier shows at the time but Whaddon might have been right about the combination of the two. The large rough Champion was Mrs Gentry's *Sally*, a well known winner. In 1986 the Whaddon Chase Hunt, losing hunting country year after year to expanding towns and major roads, amalgamated with the Bicester and Warden Hill Hunt. One more show was to be held, this time a few miles away at Stoke Hammond which turned out to be a better site than Mursley. The show, under the energetic direction of Peter Tabor, who re-started Lambourn in 1976, was better than ever and was the occasion of the presentation of the Sue Sowerby Trophy for rough lurchers, Sue having died that spring of cancer. The winner was again Mrs Gentry's *Sally* who beat John Bromiley's *Isaac*. Sadly that was the last 'Whaddon', the new, amalgamated Hunt not wishing to carry on the show.

The Lowther Country Fair, held at Lowther Castle about ten miles south of Penrith, is built around a three-day carriage driving event, one of the main annual competitions in that discipline; carriage dressage on Friday, the marathon driving on the Saturday and obstacle driving on the Sunday. Also on offer are the usual contents of a 'country fair', clay pigeons, gun dog trials and demonstration, terrier show, hound show, for Lowther is in Fell Hound country, a hound trail, fly fishing and many other attractions. There are many hardy lurcher men in the North West, from Lancashire and West Yorkshire, through Cumbria and over the Borders into Scotland and in 1976 a lurcher show was added to the Sunday programme. For this and the next four years the ring was far too small and sited at the top of the bank above the trade stands; those who judged had to cope with competitors double and even treble-banking round the ring. The show was popular and well attended with many good dogs being shown. In 1982 the lurcher show organiser, Maurice Salkeld, got a fresh site for the lurchers east of the car park where the Hound Show takes place on the Saturday. At last he was able to make the ring big enough and, what was more, with the ring on a slope one was able to weed out the dogs with bad shoulders by making them trot downhill. I judged in that ring in 1983 with 400 entries including some very nice dogs indeed. There were three height divisions, up to 22 inches, 22 to 25 inches and over 25; as almost always happens the Champion came from the middle division and was Mr R. Dempster's *Jay*, a powerful smooth brindle dog with a lovely free movement.

In previous years there had been a certain amount of poaching with lurchers on the Lowther estate at the time of the Country Fair but no more than any other very large estate has to cope with all the year round; for this reason there had been threats of stopping the lurcher show. In 1983 there was only one poaching incident that I heard of and it was dealt with promptly by local lurcher people. Nevertheless, at about 5.30pm on the Sunday evening – I was still judging in the lurcher ring – the voice of the landowner was heard over the public address system saying that 'everyone was welcome back next year except those lurcher people'! Another show, with entries somewhat less than Lambourn but equal to Whaddon and just as well run and enjoyable, had stopped. From 1971 onwards lurcher people have in many ways been their own worst enemies but in this case they had not been in the wrong They had been given another bad name due to local prejudice.

On to some of the other shows I remember, in no particular order.

In 1975 there was no show at Lambourn but there was a small show at Addlestrop, near Chipping Norton. 1976 saw the re-birth of Lambourn on its own date, the first Sunday in September. In addition there were lurcher shows at the Newton Blossomville Country Fair and at the Deane Park Country Fair and those knowledgeable lurcher owners the Jenkins family started the Badby Show. Badby ran very successfully as the Midland Lurcher Show until either 1980 or 1981 when Nick Jenkins decided that shows were doing lurchers no good and Badby stopped. There were many then and now who agreed with him.

1977 saw the start of the Tidworth Lurcher Show. It began well and seemed to have a good future. I judged there in 1978, making Tony Mills' *Biff* the Champion. He was a medium sized, rough coated wheaten dog and one of the most powerful movers of his time with tremendous thrust from the stifle, where the power should appear to come from. It may have been Tidworth's bad luck but in 1979 the weather forecast was wrong and very cold drenching rain arrived as Roger Upton started judging. The administration had tailed off, the announcer seemed to be incapable of doing his job, when the time came for the Championship judging two of the class winners were in the bar out of the rain and did not re-appear; I do not believe that the show was put on again. As I've already said, a much more successful start this year was the Whaddon as was the South and West Wilts Hunt Supporters at Fonthill which is still running. In August of that year I judged at a very nice show at Denholm, near Hawick, with some high class dogs present and also at the lurcher show at Holkham Park Fair, run with incredible efficiency by Andrew Cuthbert and his helpers in their red stockings. Holkham is a wonderful site for a 'Fair' and on the first occasion I went there one had no difficulty in getting in, walking round freely without being crowded and getting away without any traffic jam; I was later astonished to hear that the attendance that year was almost the same as the Game Fair. The lurcher show was organised by Tony Mills and it was here that he first started speed-jumping down a line of fences, in this case straw bales, against a stop watch. A hazard at Holkham was the herd of fallow deer which was still loose in the park. No lurcher actually chased one but there were several near-things not only during the racing but even when I wanted to see the two finalists move and asked their handlers to take them out of the ring and remove collars. At the last moment someone shouted 'Stop', just in time as a fallow buck galloped past only fifty yards away; knowing the two dogs there would have been a nasty mess in the car park towards which the buck was making.

1979 saw several good shows started which are no longer run. Amongst them was the Hampshire Longdogs, a very good show indeed, run at Tweseldown Racecourse, near Farnham. This was started by Michael and June Collins, who won the 1987 Waterloo Cup with 'Mousetail', to raise funds for the Alresford Coursing Club. I judged that first year and the Judges' lunch would have put a five star restaurant to shame. This was the first time I saw Roy Ware's *Shep*, who arrived too late for his class; I believe that to date *Shep* has accounted for over 50 foxes on Hayling Island. I judged there again in 1981 when the show secretary had changed and although I had one of the best Ring Stewards I'd come across in Mrs Julie Benison, the organisation had slipped a bit and the show did not last much longer. Admittedly, I heard that the final straw was a fight between some gypsies in which a car was set on fire but I cannot trace the date of the last show.

The Cottesmore Hunt Supporters show was held at a most magnificent site at Burley on the Hill; It was a most cheerful show and very well run. I had the pleasure of judging there in 1980 when the Champion was George Smith's well known brindle bitch *Eve* who I had made Champion at Holkham, and I remember being called in as referee in another year when the judges could not agree. Unfortunately the day came when the committee assumed that the very efficient organiser would run the show yet again on her own; she didn't and the show stopped.

The Heythrop Hunt Supporters ran a very enjoyable show for some years at Farmington; again, I have a note of a super Judges' lunch at Captain and Mrs Barrow's house! The day included a lurcher show, terrier show, clay pigeons, welly-throwing, a catapult range and 'guess the weight of the longhorn bull'. I judged there in 1979, the first show, with Leesa Sandys-Lumsdaine – one person I would happily judge with as our ideas on lurchers seemed to coincide – and we made Robert Newall's smooth black bitch, *Kauli*, Champion. A good small country show was held at Wappenham, in South Northants, for several years until fighting spoiled things for everyone and the landowner refused to have another show on his land.

Lurcher shows are run for various purposes and one in aid of a church roof – 'dry rot' – was held for two years at Whalton near Morpeth, run by Mrs Pat Blackett, well known as a gundog trainer and writer on gundog matters under the pseudonym of Veronica Heath. I had the pleasure of judging there in 1980 and met a high class line-up of dogs. I wrote at the time, 'the further north the better the feet' but apparently I had to revise the thought when I looked at dogs at Lowther later in the year. I well remember deciding the overall winner at Whalton by asking the finalists to jump their dogs over a garden wall and back again. The wall was some four foot high and topped with immense slabs of stone, nearly a yard across. Only one dog obeyed orders, over and back again with ease and that became the Champion; sadly, I have no record or photo of man or dog. The weekend was memorable for me as I was invited to talk about lurchers and deer poaching to the North East Branch of the British Deer Society. It was a very interesting evening indeed and I learnt a lot more than I imparted.

The Newmarket Lurcher Show was started in 1979 at the Rowley Mile Grandstand by Mr and Mrs Harrison of the Plantation Stud at Exning; it was run in aid of Riding for the Disabled and it continued there until 1984. It was a well run and enjoyable show and was attended by a larger number of travellers than most other shows bar Lambourn but unlike Lambourn there was never any trouble. In 1985 the Newmarket Show was re-started by John Bromiley on the George Lampton Playing Fields at the other end of the town. This gave more room than the Rowley Mile site and the show leaned more towards coursing, there being classes for greyhounds and whippets in addition to the usual lurcher classes. When showing was finished the racing started with a Cup for greyhounds, who were slipped in pairs by Gary Kelly in his slipper's uniform of red coat. The greyhounds were followed by whippets and then lurchers in their various sizes. Again, I never heard of any trouble at this show bar the lout who tried to snatch the car park money from a lad while the grown-up at the gate was looking the other way.

A potentially promising show was started by the king of hunting photographers, Jim Meads, at Westbury near Brackley in 1985. This show appeared to have everything in its favour; a good site on an old airfield with car parking on the concrete runways, an efficient organisation and no other show for more than a hundred miles on that day but it never really flourished and when Jim Meads moved from Westbury to Wales the show stopped. A one-off show that I enjoyed was run by Nick Scutt at Fontwell Park racecourse in 1983. It was well run by lurcher people and was notable for a five-star Judges' lunch. I mention such things elsewhere but it is always a privilege to be asked to judge at a show, specially if the show is well run, and to be given a first class lunch as well is something that remains in the memory when, perhaps, dogs are forgotten. I may have my priorities wrong but one looks at many hundreds, perhaps thousands, of dogs through the lurcher show season and a change from sandwiches is always welcome; if the change is cold pheasant and sparkling white wine, as it was at Fontwell, then hurrah for the organisers!

A very good north country show is that run by the Buccleuch Hunt Supporters at Ancrum. Apart from the wonderful scenery 'the natives are friendly', or most certainly were when I judged there in 1983. The fact that Leesa Sandys-Lumsdaine, one of the original Lambourn organisers and with whom I had judged on several occasions, and Christine Scott-Plummer, lurcher owner and Joint-Master of the Buccleuch, were the organisers promised that it would be a good show and it certainly was. I had not been warned that an Obedience Class was included and I had to make up tests on the spot; one of these was sending dogs over some iron railings into a small paddock by the ring. Up to this class the paddock had apparently been empty and I had my back to it when I asked the first dog to perform. Looking round as she cleared the fence – and jumped straight back – I found that half a dozen Blackface tups had come out from behind a shed and were grazing three or four yards away. Luckily there was no clash and the obedience test continued. The winner of that class was a very sharp smooth-coated black bitch who had given a sparkling display of immediate and enthusiastic obedience to quietly given commands. Although she had only been 4th in her show class I had no hesitation in making her the Reserve Champion. She was owned by a Mr Blair but unfortunately I have no record of her name; nor, indeed, of the Champion and owner.

A country fair that includes a lurcher show is that at Newton Abbott, held on the racecourse. I only went to it once when I judged in 1984. The entries were poor, though there were some nice dogs amongst them, the ring was a long way down the course and there were guns going off nearby, I forget whether they were muzzle loaders or clay-pigeoners. The lurcher show organisers complained of lack of advertising. I have not been to Newton Abbot again and it may have improved.

Of the shows I know, two south country events stand out, the Leconfield, Chiddingfold and Cowdray Hunt show run by Mrs Crookhall at the Kennels at Petworth since since 1980 and the shows, at various places, run by the Sussex Longdog Association. The Petworth lurcher show is not big by the standards of some shows nor are there any 'other activities' such as racing or jumping; the presence of a large herd of fallow deer in Petworth Park means that dogs, particularly lurchers, must be kept on leads; but the show is always worth attending as I have done on several occasions having been born in the area and knowing people round about. I had the pleasure of judging there in 1982 when Phil Loyd's *Lucy* was the Champion, having been Champion at Lambourn the previous year. Another year which I remember was 1985 when Mick Cawley – owner of *Queenie*, the 1982 Lambourn Champion – was judging in such monsoon-like rain that at times one could hardly see across the ring. The Champion was Donald Ralph's *Tess*, from the Sussex Longdogs; I took off my soaking wet hat to all concerned, judge, ring steward and competitors, though they could at least take shelter in between classes, and particularly to Mrs Crookhall and her helpers for keeping things going. The last Petworth I attended was in 1987 when I judged again. It has always seemed curious to me that although entries are never very big at Petworth one can always rely on seeing at least one exceptionally good class, usually either large rough or smooth bitches, lurchers that could win, and have already won, anywhere. That year I had the Ralph's *Tess*, Mrs Walch's *Amy* and several other well-known winners in the smooth bitch class.

I first saw the Sussex Longdogs Association when, together with Wyn and Delyth Jones from furthest Wales, I judged their show at Ardingly in 1983. I forget why it was on a Saturday, postponed from a Sunday, but for that reason the show entries were not enormous. I was very impressed with the way the racing was run, up a 500 yard straight course with all dogs wearing muzzles. I next saw the Club in 1986 when I attended their show at Firle, as part of the Southdown Country Fair. There were good entries and the greyhound and whippet classes were very competitive; I didn't agree with the Judges' lurcher Champion but that was their opinion on the day, not mine. The racing was, once again, of a very high standard. My third visit to the Sussex Longdogs Association was when I judged their show, with Phil Lloyd, as part of a country fair (I think) near Lewes. The site was very crowded indeed and all sorts of extraordinary events were going on, including morris dancing next door to the lurcher rings at one stage, but the lurcher entries were of their usual high standard; when it came to the final line-up we had no hesitation in making Mrs Ralph's *Tess* the Champion. The Sussex Longdogs Association run very good shows and even better racing and I hope and trust that they continue to do so.

Moving from one well-run Club to another, I saw the Herts Working Terrier and Lurcher Club at St Albans in 1985 and the first thing I noticed was the very efficient sign-posting on the M10 and the A450. It is a part of the country that can be muddling to those who like me live rurally. The Club used a rugby ground for its shows and the rings were placed in a square so that one could see at a glance what was going on. The organisation was first class, the Ring Stewards were quick and efficient and there were enough public address announcements to get classes into the rings and then blessed silence, unlike some shows where the loudspeakers are never silent. With Mr Holland from Northampton and Mr Gray from Coleshill judging, the overall Champion was Mrs Barnes' *Bruce*. In 1986 I had the pleasure of judging at St Albans with Bill Adams, MRCVS and Joint-Master of the South Shropshire – and lurcher man – doing the under-23s. Out of a hot final line-up the Champion was Mrs Morgan's *Asti*, from Chelmsford. I was sorry to see that the Herts WTC show was absent from the 1988 list and not being run in 1989.

A show that I thought had promise and which I am glad to see is still on the 1989 show list was the Welland Valley, at Hallaton; a lovely site for a show even though some of the field was ridge and furrow. In the end the Champion was Mr Helm's *Tina*, from Bestwood, and the Reserve was Mr Moody's *Fly* but it was unfortunate that the final judging was marred by a really childish display of *prima donna*-ish tantrums by the two judges who could not agree between large and small. It was embarrassing both to the organisers and to the owners of the dogs concerned and it was quite unnecessary. In the end a referee had to be called in to settle things as the judges seemed incapable of doing so.

I have twice judged lurcher shows in Wales. The first was at Glynclydach in 1984 where the show was run by the Welsh Lurcher Club in the person of Brian Peters. I was very kindly given a room at the hotel in front of which the show took place and it was only by insisting on going to bed before the sun rose on Sunday morning that I was able to look at lurchers that day with a reasonably clear head and eye. It was very hot indeed but there was an occasional breeze, the setting was marvellous and Welsh hospitality more than made up for the heat. There were four rings, up to 21 inches, 21 to 23, 23 to 25 and over 25 inches; it was interesting to see how the entries split up and the results confirmed my belief that the best lurchers are the medium sized ones.

The second visit to Wales for me was in 1988 at the Welsh Game Fair at Llandeilo, run by Adrian Simpson, *Daergi* of *Shooting News*. This time I managed to get to bed before midnight but my room was over the bar which appeared to have an all-night extension. Phil Lloyd and I were sharing the judging, doing the puppies together and then splitting with small and large until the final line-up. Both rings were on a slope, mine being fairly steep which always helps one to find out the dogs with bad shoulders, but the whole area sloped, main ring and all. A rough bitch that particularly took my eye, and who won the large rough bitch class, turned out to have come from my next-door village. We had to do the final judging for the championship in the main ring, not something that I enjoy, so as we had done at another country fair at Brockenhurst in 1987, we did the judging, chose the Champion and then moved to the main ring to repeat the process as if it hadn't already happened. The actual Champion was the large smooth bitch class winner, a curious pale grey-red brindle and a really beautiful mover.

I have always been in two minds about lurcher shows at country fairs but one I could not criticise was that held at Weston Park in 1986 where the dog side, terriers and lurchers, was very efficiently run by Ian Rainbow and the Fell and

Moorland Working Terrier Club, as one would expect. After others had judged the various classes I had to judge for the 'Champion of Champions' with £200 at stake; I comment on this business of 'Champion of Champions' on a later page. In the event I was faced with 21 lurchers each of which had won at least one championship that summer, several of them with five or six championships under their belts and with the exception of one dog who should never have won anything anywhere (an obvious saluki cross whose knees rubbed together and whose feet turned out at 45 degrees) they looked like (show) champions. It so happened that I knew of the working abilities of several of them. In the end John Bromiley's *Isaac* got the title with Mrs Samuel's *Lady*, bred by David Gaydon, as reserve.

Without turning this into a 'gazetteer' of lurcher shows I cannot mention every show that I have been to but to add a few more to the list, the Oakley started their show at the Kennels at Melchbourne, a somewhat cramped site which later changed to a bigger field at Newton Blossomville. Though the wind whistles cross the water meadows from Olney it is a very pleasant show and competently run; their new site at the point-to-point course may well be their best site so far. Another Hunt show I enjoy when I can get to it is the Atherstone at High Cross, again competently run but sometimes suffering from adjacent shows taking what could be their entries. The Grafton used to run a good show at Greens Norton but it became 'discontinued'. The Royal Agricultural Beagles run a show at Cirencester and I well remember judging at the Woodland Pytchley in 1982 with another first class Ring Steward, Jennie Evans, wife of the Kennel Huntsman.

In 1981 Tony Kirby, of the National Working Terrier Federation, and at the time B.F.S.S. Yorkshire Regional Secretary, ran a good lurcher and terrier show at Harrogate on the Show ground, not, of course, combined with the prestigious working terrier show that takes place during the Great Yorkshire Show in July but as The Northern Lurcher and Working Terrier Show in September. With the showground facilities available it was an excellent site, being enclosed by metal fences which mitigates against trouble makers and with rings, hard standing and cover already in place. After dealing with such large numbers at Lambourn a fortnight before I was relieved not to have enormous numbers to judge but the standard was high, as one would expect from Yorkshire. Expecting that there would be some racing whippets at the show and knowing that Northern racing dogs are larger than those in the South (and that many of them are cross-bred with some greyhound blood in them) I thought that there might be trouble about dogs over the mark in the 'small' classes. When those classes came into the ring many of the entries were of the racing-whippet type and it looked to me as if 75 per cent were over the mark. However, no one complained or said anything so I kept quiet and took care to pick winners at the correct height. The show was run in 1982 with Maurice Salkeld and Bob Auty judging and in 1983 Bob Auty again judging joined by Gerry Wood. But after a B.F.S.S. personnel change the lurchers were dropped. This was a great pity as Lowther also finished in 1983 and it left a gap in a great lurcher catchment area.

The Claro Beagles run a good 'Dog Day' at Rudding Park which includes lurchers and is well worth attending. It was there that I saw three policemen with their dogs come out of the main ring after their display and shepherd some fifteen hooligans out of the ground with no bother at all; it was very impressive and I have mentioned it elsewhere at slightly greater length under 'Trouble at Shows'.

The now-defunct Thames Valley Lurcher Society ran some shows at Slough in aid of Lurcher Rescue. This was, and most definitely still is a good cause and I believe that a number of lurchers were 'rescued' but the administration did not appear to have the knowledge or backing that the various pure-breed club rescue committees have and the scheme faded out, as did the T.V.L.S. after bitter recriminations following the S.N.U.K. Championship Show at Towcester. The successors, in Tony Diprose and Denis Eastwood, have made their mark with their well run shows on the old Newbury Show Ground where obedience for lurchers is such a feature.

The Fernie Hunt Show may still include a lurcher show, but one has to 'mind one's back' with the many Pony Club riders milling about in all directions. A very pleasant show was run by the South Hereford Hunt Supporters at Hereford Racecourse. A racecourse can be a good show site having car parks, hard standings, lavatories, etc. available and these were put to good use at Hereford though the parade ring may well be one of the smallest in the country. This show does not appear in current show lists though it may have been transferred elsewhere.

I have mentioned shows at 'Country Fairs'; some are successful, some not depending on whether lurcher people are running them. The main objections from lurcher owners are having to pay far too much for car parking and almost always having to park out of sight of the show rings with dogs left unsupervised in cars and vans.

The question of a show for a champion of champions is not an easy one to answer. To be realistic, such a show should come at the end of the show season, perhaps in October – though a few shows are held during the winter in indoor premises – and be open to dogs that have won a championship at any show in the country in that year and to no others, but no such show has so far been run. The reasons are various but in the end boil down to personality-clashes; several organisations consider that they, and only they, are the ones to run a final show but it never really comes off. The biggest 'Championship' show that I have been to was the *Shooting News* U.K. Finals, sponsored by *Shooting News* and held at Towcester racecourse in September 1985. I wrote at the time (in *Shooting Times*), 'It was notable not only for the number of lurchers and their owners who attended but also for the fact that the show was run by eight lurcher clubs collaborating. That there were undercurrents cannot be denied but, for the period of the show, commonsense prevailed and antagonisms – so very unnecessary in the context – were kept in abeyance for the day. Given that much accord and the very hard work put in by many people, together with a fine day and the setting, at the top of the racecourse, it was a day to remember with pleasure.' The eight clubs collaborating were the H.O.E.L.S., N.L.R.C., T.V.L.S., Norfolk, South Yorkshire, Dunmow, Midland Working Whippet Club and the Welsh Lurcher Club, Brian Peters running the actual rings with his usual firm-handed efficiency. Apparently 1,200 cars came through the gate, the furthest traveller being from Aviemore, a round trip of 950 miles. There were some 700 show entries and another 250 taking part in the racing, lure-chasing, obedience and jumping, making the overall entries in the region of 1,000. I do not know how many more lurchers there were that did not take part in anything. It was remarkable that with such a crowd of lurcher people the only damage caused was broken windows of a tractor shed at which boys were caught throwing stones for something to do.

The show was in two parts, firstly four height rings for dogs that had not qualified by winning a show that year. These winners went on to join dogs already qualified. The same four height divisions and rings were used but four fresh judges sorted them out. Thus the 16 dogs that appeared in the ring for the championship were the chosen of eight judges on the day as well as having been picked out at previous shows. They were, of course, of mixed heights from under 19 inches to over 26 inches. I had the problem of judging them and, as so often before, I found the two winners from the middle sized dogs, Mrs Gentry's *Sally* being the Champion and Mr Vigor's *Joe* the Reserve Champion. Although there were later troubles over the show administration, it was, on the day, extremely successful. If it could be done once it could surely be done again but if it has, I have not heard about it.

Chapter 2

RUNNING A LURCHER SHOW

When I wrote 'Lurchers and Longdogs' in 1976 I included a chapter, (Chapter 12), on running a lurcher show and, after thirteen more years of watching and judging at shows, it still seems to make some sense. The main requirements are picking a date that does not clash with another local show, copious advertising, particularly for new shows, realistic entry fees for cars and for dogs, allowing car parking by the rings so that owners can watch their dogs – dog stealing is still a problem – making the rings big enough, getting good ring stewards and starting at the scheduled time.

Established shows have their dates and they are part of the current lurcher summer. Until 1986 *Shooting Times* printed a list of terrier and lurcher show dates in the early Spring and weekly thereafter repeated the shows for the next ten days or fortnight; every one knew where to look and, moreover, it was free publicity. On a change of Editor in September, 1986, *Shooting Times* decided that it would only recognise gundogs and all other dogs and hounds should be banished from its pages. Many people, including me for obvious reasons, thought that this was a misguided and short sighted action. At the time of writing, lurchers are added to the official working terrier show list, at least for those show organisers who send in the required proforma in time; those who make up their minds about having a show after the beginning of the year miss the free advertising of being on the list, as do some lurchers-only shows. There is no other *reliable* and countrywide list available but the future may bring something better.

For established shows the best form of advertising is for people to visit every show within 100 miles in the three or four weeks before their own show, handing out 'rone'od' schedules. Details should be sent to whatever magazines are currently trying to cater for lurcher people with the hope that the details are printed correctly.

Entry fees must be low enough not to put people off but high enough to make a profit; £1 to £2 per car and 50p per dog seem to be the acceptable amounts at present.

Parking round and close by the ring(s) is essential. Dog stealing is, sadly, still a fact of life, many people have to leave dogs in cars and vans while they are in the ring themselves but so long as the car is within sight there is less worry.

For some twelve years or more I have written about the size of rings, exhorted organisers to make rings big enough; I have implored, beseeched and prayed but still one finds rings too small. At Kennel Club shows the ring size does not really matter; conformation and the breed standard is everything. Lurchers should be judged on movement first, balance second and conformation third and judges must be able to watch dogs walking freely round the ring. Once again I give the *rule of thumb* which is a minimum of three yards per dog round the ropes for the over-23-inch classes. Small classes can be brought inwards if necessary but there must be room for the largest expected class to walk round without treading on each other's heels or even double-banking.

Starting at the scheduled time is such an elementary matter that it should not be necessary to mention it, but time and again one hears organisers say, 'People are still arriving so we'll wait fifteen minutes or so.' Of course people are still arriving because so many shows wait for them. People who arrive late have only themselves to blame; they should have left home early enough. A cause of late starting can be the method of taking entries. I remember going to a show run by the R.A.C. Beagles which was scheduled to start at midday; at five minutes to one I asked one of the organisers when they were going to start. Pointing to the queue at the horsebox he explained that entries were still being taken. When I went to look I found that one person was solemnly writing down the name and address – and telephone number – of each competitor but no one could explain what everyone's address was needed for when I enquired. If entries are to be taken before classes go into the ring, all that is needed is the name of the dog; if there is still a queue when the first class is nearly due in the ring someone should call for entries for that class only; later classes can be dealt with once the first class has started.

If entries are to be taken before competitors enter the ring there must be some method of checking that entry fees have been paid. One method is for dog's names to be written down on a separate sheet of paper for each class which the ring steward collects and from which he checks people into or in the ring. The other is to use cloakroom type tickets which are given up on entering the ring; the objection is that unless different colours are used – and in how many colours are such tickets printed? – the ring steward does not know whether a person is in the correct class.

The simplest method of all is for the ring steward to collect entry fees as competitors enter the ring; a possible objection is that he does not know in advance how many dogs should be present, but this does not matter very much.

The choice of a Ring Steward(s) is very important. He – or, obviously, she – has to keep things running smoothly. He should be a person of some authority, or able to assert some authority. He should be like the Centurian, who said to this man come, and he cometh, and to that man go, and he goeth; or at least one hopes that he goeth. I have only once, as a ring steward, had to tell someone who was making a nuisance of himself to leave the ring; I'm glad to say that he left without further argument.

While on the subject, show organisers must consider the problem of trouble and how to deal with it if it occurs. If there has to be a beer bar it should be as far as possible from the show rings. Some shows do depend on sales, or part profit, from the bar for their takings, but, if possible, the solution is to do away with the bar altogether. Unfortunately, alcohol is portable, whether it be already inside the person or whether in bottles and tins. At that good show, the Claro Beagles Dog Day, at Rudding Park, near Harrogate, they had previously had trouble from drunks and in 1986 had done away with the bar. All went well until about 2 o'clock when about 18 hooligans arrived having obviously had a liquid luncheon. They started barging about and pickaback fighting, knocking into people and in one case falling into the terrier ring. In the main ring the Police Dog demonstration was coming to its close; the three policemen saluted, turned to their right and marched out of the ring with their dogs. Not pausing, they formed up on the far side of the hooligans and shepherded them out of the grounds. No dog was let off its lead but I was pleased to see one lout, more fool-hardy than his fellows, or perhaps more drunken, rush at a dog and shake his fist at it. He left the ground with blood running from his finger tips. The moral is that local police should at least be aware that the show is to take place.

Another problem that unfortunately has to be thought about by those who run lurcher shows is dog stealing. It has always been a fact of life though mainly in towns, particularly London in the last century. A dog would be stolen from a house in the fashionable parts of London and offered back to the owner in exchange for a sum of money; now it is usually people who are abducted, the sum demanded is vastly more and the process is called blackmail. The term 'dog fancier' came to mean a man who fancied other people's dogs. Since lurcher shows started dog stealing has been a constant worry. Cars and vans have been broken into, dogs have been taken from where they have been tied up. At one Lowther Country Fair the car park officials and the police were alerted in time to stop a car containing a stolen dog but unfortunately this does not often happen. Only recently I heard the story of a lurcher show held in a pub car park where the bar was open all day. There were many drunks, including a small gang of tinkers who were pestering people and asking if their dogs were for sale. Just before the puppy class was called into the ring one of the tinkers came up to a small boy holding a puppy on a lead and said, 'It's all right, Son; I've given your Dad the money', picked up the puppy, slipped off the collar, threw the puppy into a car and drove off, leaving the small boy in floods of tears, holding the lead and empty collar. The site being an open car park there was no one at a gate who could be alerted to stop the thief. The only safeguard, if it can be called such a thing, is to allow car parking round the ring, or rings, so that dog owners can keep an eye on their vehicles even if they are in the ring themselves. This was one of the objections to Lambourn Mk III at Newbury Racecourse where cars and vans had to be parked in the car park which was separated from the stands and rings by an eight foot high wall, very much out of sight.

On the subject of dog stealing, an old friend told me about an attempt on the part of tinkers to steal several of his dogs. At the time he employed a local teenager, a potentially very good long distance runner, to exercise some of his dogs on the local side roads. One day the lad was out with some half dozen lurchers doing his ten miles on the road when a tinkers' van drew up alongside him. They asked him if the dogs were for sale and he said that they would have to ask Mr Smith, at such and such an address. Thanking him, the tinkers drove off. Some fifteen minutes later when he was about two miles from home, the van drew up alongside him again and the driver said, 'I've seen Mr Smith and I've paid for that smooth brindle bitch'. The other man in the front of the van then said, 'And I've paid him for the dark rough dog and we'll take them now'. The boy having his wits about him said that he was sorry but he had no authority to hand over any dogs to anyone and started trotting on for home. At that moment a tractor towing a muck spreader appeared out of a gate and turned towards the village and the boy ran along in front of it with the dogs until the tinkers gave up the pursuit.

I could write on about case after case of dogs being stolen from houses, from yards, from kennels but the facts are too well known in the lurcher world. There are always those who would rather steal than breed or even buy. Anti-theft devices can be installed, guard dogs can be kept – but even they can be poisoned or distracted by a bitch on heat – but constant vigilance is the only answer and even that is not infallible. For the owner, the truly awful thing about a stolen dog, or the dog that is lost, is not knowing what has happened to it; is it still alive, is it being looked after or has it been abandoned again?

The showing classes have not really changed since the first Lambourn Show in 1971. They are Rough Dog, Rough Bitch, Smooth Dog and Smooth Bitch; these are either preceded or followed by Puppies and followed by Veterans. What may differ from show to show is the height division, or divisions.

When shows started the division between large and small lurchers was at 22 inches. By about 1977 people began to realise that the numbers over and under 22 inches were very uneven and most shows changed the division to 23 inches. This evened entries out so that where there were two judges, one doing the 'small' and one the 'big' classes, they had more equal numbers to deal with. One occasionally comes across more divisions, particularly where a show is advertised as a 'Champion of Champions' or similar. In 1985 the Welsh Lurcher Club at Glynclydach divided at under 19 inches, 19 to 23, 23 to 25 and over 25 inches, thus giving four heights. I have seen other shows do this – I think the last Lowther Show was one – and the overall winner has always come from the 23 to 25 inch group, the medium lurchers.

Puppies should always be put on the schedule as from 6 to 12 months of age. People will 'Ooh' and 'Aah' when they see a small child dragging a small puppy round the ring but one cannot seriously judge a four month old puppy against a 10 or 11 month old. Veterans should be 10 years and over. One often sees Veteran classes at 'Over 6 years' or 'Over 7 years' but these dogs should still be working. A Veteran is over the age of regular work though many of them still give good service.

At the end of the usual show classes comes the Championship, or Championships. That is to say, the winners of the various Large Classes for the Large Champion and the winners of the Small Classes for the Small Champion. Personally I do not like an overall Championship, the Large Champion versus the Small Champion and I believe it to be wrong.

At the larger Kennel Club shows there will be Group judging where the winners in the various Groups are brought back into the ring to be judged for Best of Group. For instance, for the Hound Group, in come the Champions of the Deerhounds, Greyhounds, Whippets, Salukis, Wolfhounds, Bassets, Dachshunds (standard and miniature), Beagles, Borzois, etc. The appointed judge will be an All-rounder who is qualified to judge all the breeds that appear in front of him and he will judge them, NOT by their suitability to do their original work but against the Standard laid down for each breed. He will judge according to a written Standard and not from his own knowledge of what is required of, say, the Deerhound in catching a deer in mountainous country or of the Saluki in catching a gazelle in the Arabian deserts. One doubts whether as much as 0.1 per cent of present day all-round Kennel Club judges have such knowledge. Nevertheless, he will award the rosettes and he may well put the miniature Dachshund above the Deerhound, not because it looks to him more capable of bolting a badger than the Deerhound of pulling down a stag but because it conforms more to the Dachshund Standard than the Deerhound does to the Deerhound Standard.

For lurchers there is no 'Standard'. The lurcher judge judges, or should judge, by deciding which of the dogs in front of him *looks* most capable of catching hares or rabbits and going on doing so. He will, or should, make up his mind from the movement, balance and make and shape of the dogs in the class. When all the scheduled classes have been judged, the winners come back into the ring for the judge to pick out the best of them. If it is the over-23-inch section he looks for the best hare dog (if he has foxes and deer in his mind as well that is up to him); if it is the under-23-inch section he is probably looking for a dog for ferreting or hedging. I don't mention lamping because really good lamping dogs come in all sizes. So, at the end of the day there are two Champions, one for hares and the other for rabbits to put it at its simplest. They are different dogs for different jobs and I have always thought it wrong that one should be given a further prize above the other. The serious lurcher man picks his dog according to the work he wants it to do. If, for instance, he lives in an intensive farming area with small fields and many hedges he will not look for a 27 inch greyhound-saluki cross that will run all day in Norfolk or Lincolnshire but is lost in close country. There were, and perhaps still are, some Shows that realised this difference and do not award an overall Championship. One was Whaddon where they had separate Championship Trophies for Large Rough, Large Smooth, Small, and Puppies and left it at that.

Another objection to an overall championship is the fact that when two judges are employed, one for the large classes and one for the small, putting them together to judge the overall Champion almost inevitably results in a compromise. They are not judging against a Standard; all they can say is, 'That, in my opinion, is the best of the large/small classes'. If they know their job they will both be right. If one judge is a stronger character than the other he will probably get his way. Otherwise, with the four or more class winners in front of them, they will argue for a bit and then one will probably say 'I'll agree to your Rough Dog/Bitch as Champion but I want the Smooth Bitch as Reserve'. Occasionally the two judges cannot agree and I have already mentioned watching this happen with the two judges flouncing around the ring and behaving like *prima donnas*. It was embarrassing for everyone else, particularly the owners of the two dogs and not least for me as I was called in as referee. If there are two judges, one for the large classes and one for the small and the show organisers have *got* to award an overall championship then they should nominate a separate judge or referee beforehand to do the final judging; but provided that the two dogs are good of their type he can only give his opinion according to his own preferences. When I have had to do this myself I have always tried to pick the dog that would keep me in grub if I was living rough.

In addition to the usual show classes there are others that can be added. One usually meets with a Pairs Class; the Family Group can be any number but should include at least one parent. The Working Group is 2 Large Lurchers, 1 Small Lurcher and 1 Terrier as a minimum, handled by one person. I have seen as many as ten dogs in a Group, but the important point is that there should be at least 2 Large and 1 Small. How the Judge deals with this lot depends on what he normally does with his own dogs and his general knowledge of working dogs, including terriers. With the Working Group I ask the handler to walk across the ring and run back; at least one lot of dogs can be relied on to get between the handler's legs and trip him up.

When the show classes are finished, and not until then, come the racing, jumping, obedience etc; whatever the show has time or space for.

After the judge, the most important person, or persons, at any dog show, whether under Kennel Club rules or not, is the Ring Steward. At lurcher shows this poor soul is, as often as not, someone who has been press-ganged into doing the job with no previous experience and no knowledge of lurchers. In fact, a knowledge of lurchers is not all that important, nor is previous experience. Much more important is common sense and the ability to exert some authority. As I have said above, he or she should be like the Centurion (Matthew, 8, 9); 'go, and he goeth, come and he cometh, do this and he doeth it'. I say 'he or she', but outstandingly the three best Ring Stewards I have had the pleasure of meeting in some 70 and more judging appointments have been women. Only one of them had done the job before and none of them kept lurchers but, oddly enough, two of them hunted. I suspect that they had both been Pony Club Commissioners for they each ran their show like clockwork; and that is how a show ought to run. Bad and idle ring stewards are a waste of time and I will not comment on some that I have seen. Above all horrors is the ring steward who talks to the judge unless he is asked a direct question; boiling in oil is too good for him.

I offer the following notes as a guide to anyone who may be asked to act as a Ring Steward at a lurcher show:

1. Get to the show ground at least an hour hour before the advertised time of starting; if you have not already been to the ground, or talked to the organiser beforehand, get there even earlier.

2. Check the system of entry. Are names taken beforehand? In a horsebox, for instance, or tent? If so, what proof will there be that entry fees have been paid? Lists of names on separate sheets of paper for each class? Cloakroom type tickets? The simplest method is to take the entry money as competitors come into the ring, but something to hold change will be needed, like the 'kangaroo pouches' that street and market traders use.

3. Check the size of the ring(s); the organisers may not be lurcher people. Remember that the rule of thumb is at least 3 yards per dog for the over-23 inch classes. This should have been agreed with the organisers before the show ground was laid out, particularly if the show is part of a country fair. People who run such things tend to think that lurcher shows only need a corner for their affairs. Remember that long grass may hide a multitude of terrible feet and there must be some form of hard surface for the judge to put dogs onto, usually in the final sorting out. The important thing is that the surface should be rough enough for dogs not to slide about on; hardboard, rough side upwards, is usually sufficient, otherwise the surface should be covered with coir matting. If you have not got an accurate measuring stick with a bubble to show the level, remind the organiser to provide one; measuring is your responsibility, not the judge's.

4. Go through the schedule and check that there are rosettes for each class; they should be in envelopes with the class number on the outside.

5. Get hold of the Judge as soon as he arrives, take him to the ring and ask him how he is going to judge:

(a) are dogs to go round clockwise or anti-clockwise?

(b) will he go round the ring looking at dogs or does he want them to come into the middle to him, one at a time?

(c) how will he line up the chosen few? If the sun is out he should have it behind him and if the ring is on a slope the dogs should be above him, but whatever he does it *must* be the same for each class, otherwise everyone gets confused. Remember that the winner is *always* at the left of the line as the Judge looks at them.

(d) tell the judge how many rosettes there are for each class and what the Championship consists of; Champion alone? Champion and Reserve?

(e) when you are happy that you know what the Judge wants, remind him of the time of start and what the first class is to be.

6. Fifteen minutes before the scheduled time of starting announce on the loudspeaker, 'Class one, rough dogs over 23 inches, into ring one in fifteen minutes',

or whatever the first class is to be. Repeat the announcement at 10 minutes to and at 1 minute to the time, say, 'Class one, rough dogs over 23 inches into ring one now, please'. If there are two Stewards, the other one should be in the ring ready to take money or check entries. When you think the class is all in, tell the Judge.

7. While competitors are walking round the ring keep them moving briskly and stop them cutting corners.

8. Keep an eye on the Judge and when you think he is about half way through go and collect the rosettes for that class. When the Judge starts calling dogs in make sure that they line up on the agreed spot. Some judges call in dogs themselves, some want the Steward to do it.

9. Having got a line-up the Judge will make his final placings. Stand behind him with the rosettes ready but do not speak to him unless he asks you a question; he should be concentrating on his job.

10. When he is satisfied the Judge will say, 'That's it', or something similar. Hand him the rosettes one by one unless he asks you to give them out. Tell the winners not to leave the ring until you have got down their names, addresses and names of dogs.

11. Remind the Judge what the next class is and then go and call them into the ring.

12. When you come to the Championship you should call in class winners by name over the PR system and get them walking round the ring *in the order of their classes.* Remind the Judge about prizes, i.e., Champion only or Champion and Reserve, etc.

13. The Judge must be offered his travel expenses; whether he takes them is up to him. It is really a matter for the organisers but some don't know and some forget; whatever happens it is embarrassing for the Judge to have to ask. The usual calculation is 'so many miles at so much mpg at so much per gallon makes £XYZ'.

14. Trouble; at one time one could expect more or less trouble from a minority. Big trouble must be dealt with by the police and you should check whether they will be available. Nowadays there does not seem to be as much trouble as there used to be but there is always the complainer. If he persists, give him his money back and ask him to leave the ring; the Judge's opinion is final. You may be asked if a dog is rough or smooth; always refer this to the Judge.

15. Finally, remember that lurcher shows go on whatever the weather, so dress accordingly. Others can get under cover when they are not in the ring but you and the Judge have got to sweat it out to the end in sun, rain or blizzard.

As I have seldom shown my own dogs – though each of them did win a championship at some time or another – it is probably presumptuous of me to tell others how to show a dog to the best advantage. Some may say 'What does it matter how I show my dog?' But from the *judge's* point of view it does matter since the judge is trying to put the best dog at the top of the line; if the judge does not get a proper look at every dog he may not get them in the right order. So, from the judge's point of view I offer some suggestions as to what, and what not to do in and out of the ring.

To start with, arrive on time. Unless you already have a copy of the show schedule try and arrive at least fifteen minutes before the advertised starting time. I know many shows start later but do not rely on a late start. Some shows start with the under 23s, some with the overs, some with roughs and some with smooths so, for instance, do not rely on the puppy classes being judged first.

Read the schedule and enter your dog in the correct class. You should know your dog's height accurately. If you are in any doubt as to whether it is rough or smooth ask someone *before* you make your entry if entries are being taken beforehand, or *before* you enter the ring if entries are being taken in the ring.

Whatever coat the dog has it should, at least, be clean. This is common sense. A daily brushing helps the general muscular condition and, with a longer coated dog, may show up some minor damage that has not been spotted. In this sense, lurcher shows *have* been good for lurchers − or some lurchers − in that one does not now see the dirty, mangey dogs that one was asked to run one's hand over fifteen years ago.

Toe nails should be trimmed to a sensible length. Over-long nails mean damaged feet in the end.

Recent damage should show signs of being treated; either stitched or at least the hair clipped round the cut or tear and the wound itself cleaned.

In the ring, keep the dog awake and on its feet. When a judge has several similar looking dogs in a class he will, when looking at one of them, often look back across the ring at others of the same type for comparison. If one or more of them are lying down while their owners have a cigarette and a gossip they may be left out of the final placings.

When the judge is looking at your dog, whether it is on grass or on the door or whatever hard surface dogs are being stood on, see that it stands naturally; do not 'stack' it, or stretch it out as is done at Kennel Club shows. The judge is, or should be, looking for balance; a good lurcher should look as if it could jump off straight into a gallop. This can be seen if the dog is standing naturally but not if it has been stretched out with its front legs too far forward, its hind feet too far back and its head hauled up into the air. Leave that to the dog show people.

Do not speak to the judge unless he speaks to you first. He, or she, is or should be concentrating on your dog. If he wants to know how old it is or how it is bred he will ask you. Above all, do *not* tell the judge how well your dog has done at other shows and how many prizes it has won or how many hares or rabbits it took last night. With some judges this may result in you being at the bottom of the line when the rosettes are handed out, however good the dog may be.

There are certain ethical principles in showing which I believe ought to be adhered to. Not many, but there are sensible reasons for them.

Never show a dog under a person who bred that dog and try to avoid showing under the person who bred its sire or dam. If the judge is honest, he will bend over backwards to avoid showing any favours to a dog that he has bred. If he is not honest he may well give you a rosette but spectators will condemn both you and him. This not an unusual situation. I have, once, given a first prize to a dog that I had bred but he was outstandingly the best in the class. All the same, I told the owner what I thought of his showing that dog under me. Unfortunately, we have all seen blatant cases of judges favouring dogs of their own breeding but it does not, in the end, do much for the reputations of those involved.

Organisers, and anyone else concerned in the running of a lurcher show, be they a judge, ring steward or whatever else, should not show any dog of their own at that show, no matter who it is handled by. Rightly or wrongly, there is always the feeling that some favouritism may have been shown.

It comes back to common sense and behaviour.

A lurcher show is a whole day out particularly if the starting time is in the morning; even with the shows that start at 1 or 2pm one may have up to a two hour journey so whether one is attending, showing or even judging there are two things that are needed during the day, lunch and loo.

Lunch is what one wants and what one makes it. Walking along the line of cars during a lunch break, or before the show starts, one sees the whole spectrum from meat pies, crisps and coke to (sometimes but not so often nowadays) picnic baskets, cold chicken and wine bottles. At one time the best sight and smell was from Tony's old blue van from Wolverhampton, with the Gaz cooker and the big saucepan into which went onions, sausages, beans, tomatoes and tins of soup, to be washed down with their home-made wine. If one is privileged to be asked to judge at the show one is sometimes told that the organisers will provide lunch. Looking back at some years of judging at lurcher shows I have been given some memorable lunches; memorable from several points of view, from peaks to troughs with plateaux in between. It would be invidious of me to give star ratings and I will not names names, other than one or two who I have already mentioned, but I cannot write about judges' lunches without including Lambourn of sad and happy memory. At Seven Barrows those superb hosts, Mr and Mrs Walwyn, provided helpers lunches of five star standard not only in quality but in quantity too. With a mid-morning start (10.30 at Lambourn) one does not always get away from the ring at lunch time, and I have always preferred to judge on until finished; but at Seven Barrows I have found a wonderful lunch still ready at 4.30pm.

A trough I remember, in the sense of the bottom, was a stale cheese bun, a can of warm beer and no glass and a damp straw bale to sit on and half way through the feast to be told that the first class was being brought foward half an hour because of the racing and was I ready? I was. On to a peak the following year with a judges' and helpers' sit-down luncheon in a baronial hall, served by a butler and two maids. A successful and enjoyable show was originally run by a charming lady who was, and I'm sure that she still is, a very good cook. Judges' lunch that year consisted of cold chicken tarragon in a cream sauce and a good white wine, chilled to perfection. Alas, she handed over to another organiser and the next time I went to that show the judges' lunch was two-day-old buns with the filling forgotten and 'Help yourself to the light ale from the crate'. No wonder that show did not last much longer!

The plateau between peak and trough is a plate of 'ham salad' on a table in the beer tent and there is usually a trough coming when one is told, 'Oh, ask at the bar will you? They've got something for you I'm sure'. It is six to four on that the bar know nothing about it. Ups and downs, good or crummy, but many more peaks than troughs and one is always very grateful for the trouble that people go to when they are extremely busy getting the show itself on the move.

Having had lunch – or having arrived for a morning's start – there is an important visit to be made before the judge spends anything up to five hours in the ring looking at lurchers. Here there has been a steady improvement since the early days but I suppose that this is inevitable with the rise in the numbers of people attending lurcher shows and man's technological ingenuity.

To begin with it was the nearest hedge, or a further one if the nearest had been cut and laid. This was all right for men, unless they were holding a lot of lurchers on leads who suddenly saw something that they wanted to chase, but not so good for ladies. Haystacks are a notch up the scale but they are rare things in the countryside nowadays and anyway the hidden side would only accommodate so many people at a time. The Hessian Mark I – a sheet of hessian nailed to four posts and held up by guy ropes until enough people have tripped over them and the whole thing falls to the ground – is not seen now as often as it once was; the Hessian Mark II had corrugated iron troughs. Next comes the wooden shed with a tin roof but it seldom has washing facilities so if one is judging a large number of dogs it is wise to carry water, soap and towel in the car. Near the top of the scale is the Portaloo; there is, or was, a wooden model high off the ground, down the steps of which elderly gents, small boys and those who had been at the bar since the beginning of the show usually fell. But even the standard model is not solid enough to withstand a hurricane. Shows which are held at permanent sites have a great advantage in that the necessary facilities are already on tap. Of course they vary but the prize must surely go to the original Newmarket Lurcher Shows held at the Rowley Mile stands; those marble basin, etc., are of Harrods quality but I was always puzzled to see from the notices that they were, apparently, for the use of I.T.V. Staff only (now Channel 4).

Chapter 3

JUDGING LURCHERS

For judges at Kennel Club shows there are written breed standards by which each breed is judged. Whether one agrees with a particular standard is another matter; those for the hounds, working breeds and terriers were, no doubt, written in the days when the dogs concerned did work but successive generations of breeders and judges have interpreted many standards to the point where the original work the dog did has been lost sight of. What bulldog of today could pin a bull by the nose and hang on? What show greyhound could catch a hare? What prize winning Dandy Dinmont could go to ground after a fox or badger? In most cases there is nothing basically wrong with the standards; it is the interpretation by judges with no knowledge or experience of working their dogs and the greed of breeders that has brought deterioration to so many breeds.

However, for lurchers there is no written standard and the judge has to rely on his own experience. The only other shows at which this is the case are hound shows. Hounds are judged by men who for six or seven months of the year spend their weekdays directing, assisting and controlling packs of anything between fifteen and forty couples of hounds in the infinitely difficult task of catching foxes, hares or deer. During the summer they spend many days at their own and other kennels looking at and talking about hounds. These men need no written standard to guide them. They believe, from experience, that hounds of a certain shape are more likely to catch foxes than another shape.

So it is with lurchers. The man who would judge lurchers must rely on his own experience of running dogs, of longdogs. He must know from practical experience that a dog of a certain shape is more likely to work than a dog of a different shape. This practical experience must be backed up by a knowledge of canine anatomy and by soaking the eye in dogs, looking critically at large numbers of dogs until an assessment is automatic; that this assessment may have to be changed on closer examination does not matter. Given enough experience, the first assessment is usually not far out.

The truth is that the good judge of one animal is usually the good judge of another, particularly where galloping animals are concerned, i.e., horses and running dogs. Such people are usually born with a stockman's eye, the eye that sees at a glance whether an animal is right or wrong. It does not matter whether the animal is a racehorse in the paddock before a race or a lurcher in the show ring. Often such people cannot immediately explain why they have seen something right or wrong; they know it instinctively. An eye for a dog means being able to take in the whole dog at a glance before one's eye and mind pinpoint the details. It means that the lurcher judge who has this sense has a very good idea of the ultimate placings by the time a class has walked once round the ring. Many a time I have thought as a dog has come into the ring, 'That's my winner so long as his feet are OK'. Over the years I have usually been right, or so nearly right that the dog has been placed to a better one.

There is one other requirement for the successful judge and that is confidence. It is true that confidence usually comes with practice but it does help if one has lived the sort of life where one has had some sort of authority or otherwise been used to performing in front of other people. The man who is used to making decisions will not dither when faced with a class of lurchers in the ring with a critical crowd standing three and four deep round the ropes.

So much for the judge himself and, when I say himself I obviously include the many women judges, some of them very good. How is he going to carry out his job?

Since he has no written standard to help him, the methods he uses do not really matter so long as every dog is examined both visually and, in part, manually. What the judge must not do is to stand in the middle of the ring and judge from a distance, as hounds are judged. Most of the complaints about judging at lurcher shows used to come under the heading of, 'He never put a hand on my dog'. The owners have paid their entry fee and every dog must be examined, no matter how terrible it is.

Next in importance to examining every entry is consistency. The judge who is consistent in his methods, whatever they are, will not miss any step and, after the first class, competitors will know what is required of them and spectators will know what to look for. Time and time again I have seen judges who have, for instance, sent the first class clockwise round the ring and have lined up the winners North and South. The next class starts anti-clockwise and the judge lets them get on with it; this time he lines up the winners East to West and puts the first dog at the right of the line. The spectators are mystified as they expected the left-hand dog to get the red rosette, and competitors in the third class stand about not knowing what to do.

As guide to the beginner I will explain my own method. It is not necessarily the best and certainly not the only method. I can only say that in the light of experience it does work. It is based on judging lurchers by

movement
balance
make and shape

in that order. Firstly *movement*, because if a lurcher cannot gallop he cannot do his job; secondly, *balance*, because if a lurcher is not naturally balanced he cannot start, stop or turn easily and will wear himself out all the quicker. *Make and shape*

35

I put third, because so long as a lurcher's basic conformation is somewhere near correct, he is balanced and he moves well there will not be much wrong with him.

Before the show starts I take the Ring Steward into the ring and explain what I am going to do and what I want him to do (I might add here that of all the many Ring Stewards I have had dealings with, outstandingly the three best were women; the two worst were one of each):

1. Each class to walk clockwise round the ring. I know that this is contrary to normal dog show practice but when I examine dogs I run my right hand over each one, walking anti-clockwise round the ring, so I want them facing me. If they have walked anti-clockwise round the ring their tails will be facing me and each dog will have to be turned round.

2. I watch the dogs walking round the ring for five or six circuits.

3. I go to a corner and watch the whole class walking towards me and then turn round to watch them walking away.

4. I go round the ring examining each dog in turn. The exception to this is if the class is less than about ten in number. Then it is sometimes better to line them up straight away and examine each dog on the 'board', or whatever hard surface has been provided.

5. I send the class round the ring again and call in the dogs I want to examine more closely. The number will depend on the general standard of dogs, the size of class and the number of rosettes on offer. With an enormous class, 50 to 100 dogs, I would pull in from 15 to 30; with a small class I pull in three more than the number of rosettes. The reason for this is that if there are three rosettes and four dogs are pulled in, one exhibitor goes out of the ring grumbling to himself. If there are three rosettes and six dogs are pulled in, then three people go out of the ring saying that the judge doesn't know what he is doing which cheers them up and they feel better for it! For this examination it doesn't matter what order the dogs stand in so long as the Ring Steward lines them up where I want them.

6. When the dogs I need are lined up – and here I would add that the judge should have the sun behind him if it is shining; and if the ring is on a slope the dogs should be above him – I have each dog onto the hard surface to see what his feet are like. I then send his owner out on a triangular course, away, across and straight back to see how the dog moves. It has always been a source of amusement, and mystification, to me to see how few people are capable of walking in a straight line. I say, 'Would you please take your dog to that corner of the ring, across that side of the ring to *that* corner and then straight back to me' and it is wonderful to see the number of people who will walk round in a circle.

7. I then send the line round the ring again and pull in the first three in what I hope is the right order, plus a certain number of doubtfuls who may, or may not, be moved up (see 5 above). The winner is *always* at the left hand end of the line as I look at them, with numbers 2, 3, 4, etc., to his right as I look at them

but, of course, on his left as he looks at them. If this is always done then the spectators know what to expect.

8. I do a final check, moving dogs up and down if absolutely necessary, and then ask the Ring Steward to hand out rosettes.

Now to the actual judging, beginning with *Movement*. There is a trick in watching a class of dogs walking round the ring, and it is to imagine that there is a wall, or other solid fence, along one side of the ring with a gap of 8 or 10 foot in the middle . Standing about two thirds of the way back across the ring I watch each dog as it crosses the 'gap'. I do not look at the dog as it approaches the 'gap' and I switch back to the next dog as soon as one has cleared the 'gap'. In this way each dog is watched for the same length of time which, after all, is only fair to them all. Often one sees a judge watching a dog halfway round the ring and then turning in another direction to watch another dog for half a circuit. This almost certainly means that some dogs are missed and it gives an unbalanced view of the class; a judge must remember that he is judging each dog against the standard *of that class*, not against a written standard.

Watch racing on television, particularly National Hunt racing, and listen to the paddock commentator, currently Jimmy Lindley or Richard Pitman, as he discusses the horses walking round. When you hear the words, '. . . and doesn't he move well', watch that horse and see the way his hind feet over-step the front feet; in other words, how much further forward the hind feet come down beyond what would have been the front foot marks if the horse was walking on a sandy or muddy surface. This over-stepping is a sure guide to the way the horse will gallop, the hind foot coming down short of the front foot mark showing a short, choppy stride and the six inch or nine inch over-step showing a long flowing stride. So it is with running dogs and over-stepping is the first thing to look for. Watch the way each dog moves its forelegs, the free, confident mover that stretches out its legs and puts its feet down crisply; free movement in front means a well-placed shoulder blade. Watch for the stifle bending as the hind leg is brought forward and see how much over-step there is. The whole movement should be supple and suent, the front legs stretching out and the hind legs moving the dog powerfully forward, the dog looking balanced and symmetrical.

When I have watched the class passing the 'gap' in the wall enough times – and it should be at least five or six circuits to see them all properly, though with a big ring and a small class the judge can turn round and watch another 'gap' on the opposite side as well, I go to a corner and watch the whole class coming towards me, then turn round and watch them all going away. Some of the good movers who I had noted from the side may turn out their front feet, some badly, and others rub their hocks together as they move away.

Having watched the class moving I now look at them for *balance* and *make and shape*. I ask everyone to stop where they are round the ring and pick a dog to start on. If the class is large it is easy to forget where one started so I pick an owner wearing distinctive clothing, a bright red sweater for instance, or a dog that is different in colour from the rest.

I walk up to the first dog from the front, watching its expression; most lurchers are naturally friendly and I like to see a dog that looks up confidently and wags its tail. One can tell a lot from this first glance about the dog's character; inevitably one does come across the odd dog that is either nervous or bad tempered. Having taken in the shape of the dog's head from the front, the next thing is to look at its teeth; with a nervous dog this can usually be done by talking to the dog and running one's hand over its head first. With the bad tempered dog I do not waste time. I ask the owner to show me its front teeth; if he gets bitten it will be his fault for bringing a bad tempered dog into the ring.

I sometimes wonder why I bother to look at lurchers' teeth, except in veteran or puppy classes. In fifteen years or so of judging I doubt if I have come across more than a dozen bad mouths a year, if that. For the other side of the coin, I remember judging the Coursing and Racing classes at a Whippet Club show some years ago; there were some 78 entries in the six classes and out of that number I found 11 bad mouths, mostly overshot. However, a dog that is undershot or overshot cannot catch and hold properly and as it is embarrassing to be told afterwards that a winner has a bad mouth it is worthwhile looking at them all.

While looking at the dog from in front I will have noticed the width of the head, particularly behind the ears. This is a good indication of brains, or lack of them; I will also have looked at the chest, front legs and feet. If I have any doubts about the front legs I will probably pick the dog up a few inches and let it drop back to the ground again; this will check whether the feet really do point forwards or outwards or whether the owner has posed the dog to hide a fault. Having looked at the teeth I run my hand over the dog's head, down the neck, over the top of the shoulder blades – making a quick measurement of their width apart, two, three or four knuckle widths? Then on down the back to see what the great muscles are like, a quick pinch of skin on the ribs as another check on fatness and to see how clean the coat is, and on to the hips. Here again, a check on width, four knuckles with the big dogs, especially the bitches, a hand down each side of the quarters and the second thigh to feel the muscles and then pull the tail up between the hindlegs and check its length. A long tail means a fast dog; with greyhound types the tail should stretch across the spine and with whippet types it should reach the spine or thereabouts. Running a hand over the dog like this has told me how fit it is, how clean the coat, whether it will stretch its head down to the ground easily and whether the hips are broad enough to carry the muscles and hind legs. As with teeth, there is the odd nervous or bad tempered dog that will not stand when I run my hand over it. Rather than have a fight, I merely examine the dog visually; I will probably not give it a rosette because of its temperament.

Now I stand back two or three yards from the dog and look at it from the side. Does the dog look balanced and symmetrical? Does it stand fore-square with a leg at each corner? Does it look as if it could jump off at a gallop from where it stands? Does it look whole, or does the front not match the rear half? The length of head usually equals the length of neck. Does the top line of the neck flow smoothly onto the back? If it does then the shoulder is well laid back. Look at the slope of the shoulder blade; to gallop properly the dog must stretch out its front legs. The joints at the point of the shoulder and at the elbow have a limited amount of free movement so, if the shoulder blade is upright and the *humerus*, the bone between elbow and shoulder, slopes backwards, the front leg will not stretch out. If the shoulder blade slopes back and the *humerus* is nearly upright the dog can stretch out its front legs and gallop.

I next look at the depth of chest, where the heart and lungs are, essential for the running dog, and then at the length from hip to hock. The greater this length and the nearer the hock to the ground the faster the dog. Finally I walk round to look at the dog from behind, to see the muscular development; then a 'Thank you' to the owner and on to the next dog.

Having examined them all I go back to the middle of the ring, look round the class to check where the dogs are that I want to bring in and then ask owners to walk on again. I go to one side of the ring and, as each dog that I want approaches, I ask the owner to turn in, leaving the Ring Steward to line them up; this will merely be in the order in which they come round. The reason I bring dogs in from the side of the ring is a final check on movement. With a small class of 10 or 15 dogs one can remember the half dozen one has picked out. With a very large class it is easy to miss a dog that may not be as impressive as some others to look at but which is a good mover, in other words it moves straight without turning its feet out or its hocks too far in. I doubt if the enormous classes of the late 1970s and early 1980s will ever be seen again but even with 30 or so one can still miss a dog.

Having got the dogs I want I say 'Thank you' to the remainder and start the final examination. Each dog in turn is put on the hard surface, whatever it may be (and here I would remind organisers that a slippery surface is useless; it must be rough enough for dogs to stand confidently), I look at their feet and then ask each owner in turn to walk his dog out, across and straight back to me; as I have already said, it is quite extraordinary to see how many people cannot walk in a straight line.

That done, I ask the owners to walk round once again — only a small circuit is needed — and I bring in half a dozen or so, depending on the number of rosettes, in what I hope is the right order. I do a last check, first from the side and then walking slowly along the line looking down at the spring of rib. It is not really a good thing to move dogs up and down at the last moment but occasionally one has to do it, particularly if two dogs are more or less equal. Sometimes it helps to ask both owners to walk their dogs side by side across the ring and back. One should not waste time at this stage — it looks as if one cannot make up one's mind — and when I'm certain of the placings I say to the Ring Steward, 'That's it'. He then gives out the rosettes, or whatever prizes there are, and takes down names of dogs, owners, addresses, etc as the show needs.

This all sounds like a very long rigmarole, but with practice and confidence it does not take long. Over the years I have found that I get through a day at the rate of about 1½ minutes per dog so long as the Ring Steward does not waste time calling in each class. Of course one can take longer over it with small classes when each class can be brought straight into the middle of the ring after their movement has been watched; there is no need to examine them by walking round the ring and then looking at them again in the centre, but with 150 or 200 dogs to look at one is beginning to talk about five hours judging, or more.

Turning from the usual four classes of rough and smooth, dog and bitch, to the extras, one has puppies, veterans, family groups, working groups; perhaps there are others as well at some shows.

Firstly *Puppies*: so long as the organisers make it clear on the schedule that the ages are from 6 to 12 months there should not be many problems. As regards height, one judges on the premise that the 'Over-23 inches' are those that will make 23 inches and over when fully grown; likewise the 'Under-23 inches' will make 23 inches or less. With the 6 and 7 month old ones it is often a matter of guess-work as to how they will turn out, particularly the ones that have a lot of growing still to do; a whippety type has usually reached its final shape, though not height, at that age. One has to take the owner's statement about age on trust but it is interesting to see how many puppies are coming up to their first birthday 'next week'!

Secondly *Veterans*: to me a veteran is 10 years old or more. In other words it is a lurcher that no longer does any serious work. All too often a schedule says 'Over 6 years' or 'Over 7 years'; this is a nonsense. If they have been reared properly and not over-run when young, a great many six and seven year olds are still working and working well and at shows they should take their chance in the normal classes. By all means have a 'Junior veteran' class if there is room and time but let the Veterans be proper Veterans. One must look at their feet and teeth and general condition, but it is heartening to see how many lurchers still look fit and well when they are past 10 years of age.

Thirdly the *Groups*; there may or may not be conditions in the schedule and one simply has to apply the conditions or use one's own judgement. If the 'Working groups' class has to consist of 'Two large, one small, lurchers and one terrier, or more' as it was originally started by Tony Mills and elaborated by me, then each group must contain what the schedule says, at least two large and one small lurcher and one terrier. I mentally compare each group to my own dogs and decide which group is most likely to work best. With family groups one has to ask which is which and who; father? mother? children? etc. Provided that they are all sound, and not cripples, judge by family likeness.

I am sometimes asked about judging between dogs and bitches. Traditionally, it was the lurcher bitches that were kept for work and for breeding; dogs were only kept if they were needed as sires. For this reason I judge on those lines. I judge the bitches as workers who will breed good litters and the dogs as possible sires, or stud dogs, that will work when needed.

So much for what, in my opinion, the judge ought to do. There are some things that he should not do.

The judge is in charge of the ring whilst judging is taking place and he must look and act as if he is in charge; the Ring Steward is there to help and keep things running smoothly. I tell the Ring Steward that measuring is his responsibility, though if a dog is obviously in the wrong class I say something about it. People ask whether a dog is rough or smooth and this must be the judge's decision. The judge's behaviour is often an indication of his worth; I would have little confidence in a judge who stands in the middle of the ring with a cigarette, or pipe, or even a cigar in his mouth and his hands in his pockets, nor in a judge who allows competitors to argue with him.

The judge should not haul dogs about unnecessarily. There is a school of judging that finds it necessary to force a dog's head downwards to see if it could pick up a rabbit and that pulls a dog's front legs out and round about to see if they are tied in at the elbow. If these people cannot tell such things by looking at a dog then they should not be judging; there are obvious physical indications of both faults. A judge should never criticise a dog to its owner unless he is asked for a criticism. I must admit that from time to time I have suggested that a dog's toenails should be trimmed but I do it quietly into the owner's ear and only then when nails are so long as to cause the dog trouble.

A common question is 'what allowance does one give for damage?' Where a cut is fresh I take no notice of it so long as it is clean and, where necessary, has been stitched. After all, lurchers are working dogs and most of them will get cut and torn sometime in their lives. Toes are another thing. I know very well that a great many dogs work on perfectly happily after having a toe down or losing a toe but a show is a 'beauty contest', whether one likes it or not, and of two dogs otherwise equal, if one has damaged toes then the sound dog must get the prize. One is often told that such-and-such a dog is a marvellous worker, no matter that his front feet stick out at 45 degrees, his hocks rub together and he is missing several teeth. The answer always is that how much better would he be if he was sound?

There are, of course, problems that the judge comes across over the years and I will give *my* solutions to some of them.

What do you, the judge, do when a very good looking dog comes into the ring that you know is gutless. You have seen it working – coursing, for instance – and you have seen it stop with the hare in sight and you knew it wasn't tired. Do you carry on as if you did not know anything about the dog? I have had this happen to me twice, perhaps three times, and in each case I left the dog concerned at the side of the ring. This may be wrong, but lurchers are working dogs or they are nothing. The reverse, when you have a dog that you know is a good worker but cannot compare with some of the others in the class for make and shape, is more difficult, particularly if you know nothing about the others. On the few occasions that it has happened to me I have judged by what the dogs looked like on the day which, considering what I have said about the bad

41

worker, is probably wrong but I comforted myself by thinking that the others might be very good workers too.

A minor problem is the question of rough or smooth; the dog that may be in the wrong class. From the showing point of view I have always gone on the principal of being somewhere near the limit if possible. Other things being equal the dog with the broken coat looks more like a lurcher than the very smooth-coated greyhound or whippet type and I would personally show it in the smooth class. From the same point of view, the dog that is 23 inches exactly is unlikely to catch the judge's eye in the over-23-inch class but it ought to do so in the under-23-inch class if it is any good.

Another problem is that of type. This may crop up if there are greyhound and whippet classes at the show as well as lurchers and I mention it because it did happen to me at a well attended show in Wales. In a class of a dozen whippets there was one black dog, larger than the others with a slightly rough coat, prick ears and a tail carried fairly high. When I pointed out to the owner that his dog looked like a small lurcher and should have been shown in the appropriate class he told me that it was a rag dog and seven eighths whippet.

While one is still judging a class it is not the time to go into long explanations. I know that a hundred years ago the terms whippet and rag dog were synonymous but in the intervening years the whippet has become an established type. To me a greyhound is a greyhound and a whippet is a whippet, both of a recognisable type. When I talk about a greyhound I mean a dog that is pure-bred and is, or can be registered in the Greyhound Stud Book or the Irish Stud Book; its breeding can be checked by looking up back numbers of the Stud Book. So, when I talk about a whippet I mean a dog that is pure bred and is, or can be registered with the Kennel Club (because of current KC regulations many breeders do not register all their produce). Its breeding can be traced and its ancestors were whippets for at least seven generations. If its breeding is not pure whippet for at least seven generations it is a whippet-type, in other words a *Lurcher*. Most people would agree that a whippet/greyhound is a lurcher; so is a whippet X whippet/greyhound (2nd generation), a whippet X whippet/whippet/greyhound (3rd generation) and a whippet X whippet/whippet/whippet/greyhound and we are now at the fourth generation but the offspring is still a lurcher. It may well be that at the Welsh show one or two of the others in the class were not pure bred but at least they looked like present day whippets whereas the black dog did not. I was prepared to believe that he was very fast and Phil Lloyd, who was judging the under-23-inch lurcher classes, might well have given him a rosette in the other ring. If the owner should ever read this page I hope that he will accept my explanation which I could not give him at the time.

There is no good horse of a bad colour and I suppose that the old saying can be applied to lurchers. But some people are prejudiced and I admit to a dislike of white dogs. Not the off-white that cream and wheaten dogs go in old age but pure white or even white with just a touch of fawn or black. I know that such a prejudice is irrational and that the old coursing belief that a hare will turn away from a white dog sooner than from a darker one cannot be proved. But the few white dogs I have had, or have known well, have all been soft; soft mentally as well as physically, compared to others of the same litter who were coloured. From the working point of view there are pros and cons. The man who is looking for game where he has not got permission to be will not use anything as obvious as a white dog. On the other hand the man who 'has permission' likes to see what his dogs are doing and a brindle or black can be almost invisible against a hedge or on plough on a dull winter day. Personally, I have always been fond of a honey or wheaten coat, though certainly not to the exclusion of fawns, brindles and blacks.

A dog showing signs of damage should not be penalised so long as it is sound but shows are *shows* and of two equal dogs, the one with no toes down should be put above the one with broken or missing toes, etc.

If one judges more than the odd show one inevitably gets to know certain dogs that are campaigned and may appear every Sunday somewhere. One puts up a good dog several times because it is the best at the show but if it is being over-shown it will almost certainly lose condition as the summer wears on. Watch for this because one is looking for the best dog *on the day*.

Lurcher people ought to be able to stand the worst of weather and lurcher shows should continue no matter how hard the wind or rain. An exception can, perhaps, be made for a thunderstorm as they seldom last long but otherwise judging should continue.

Like colour prejudice, breed prejudice is a difficult question. I don't particularly like Salukis *in this country* though, as I well know from experience, they are marvellous under desert conditions. Therefore I do tend to pass over a dog that shows too much Saluki cross if I can find a reason for doing so. Luckily, many such crosses have knees that rub together and bad feet that turn out at 45 degrees so my conscience is usually clear.

One doesn't see as many dirty and unkempt dogs as one used to do and, I'm glad to say, I haven't been asked to look at a dog with obvious skin trouble – or mange – for about ten years. But a lurcher show is a beauty show; smooth dogs ought at least to be clean and rough dogs should have had some sort of brushing before coming into the ring.

Should the judge talk to exhibitors? I pose this question because I have been asked it in the past. Kennel Club shows are very formal affairs and it is not done to drop the formality, however well one knows an exhibitor. To me, lurcher shows should not be formal beyond the point of judging as efficiently as one can and I often talk to dog owners; not to every one, though I usually ask the age of the dog. At one time I used to say 'How old?' as I walked up to each owner. More often than not the answer I got was 'Oh, hallo!' and I realised that I must be speaking indistinctly so I now say 'How old is he/she?'. Beyond that I often ask about a dog's breeding, sometimes I ask if I have seen it before if it seems a bit familiar and the occasional joke does no harm so long as it is not at someone else's expense. After all, every exhibitor has paid me a compliment by showing under me and the least I can do is to be as pleasant as I can.

As to making mistakes, a judge may make errors of judgement but they should be honest ones and he should try to officiate in a competent and polite manner whilst in the middle of the ring. The ring-side will usually forgive an error which is made in good faith but rudeness, sloppiness and bias are obvious to most exhibitors and spectators and one must always remember that whilst one is judging the dogs one is being judged oneself by the ring-side. I will instance two judging errors which are still seen too often: firstly, not handling every dog even if it is merely a matter of running a hand over the dog. Secondly, turning away from watching a dog walking or running before it has finished moving. Every exhibitor has paid his or her entry fee – if he hasn't that's up to the organisers – and the least the judge can do is to look at each dog properly, no matter how ghastly it is.

There is one other problem that a judge can be faced with: *'What's wrong with my dog?'* Sooner or later an aggrieved or merely curious owner asks this question. If there is plenty of time I suppose one could go into a detailed examination of the dog but there is seldom time to do so at a show, particularly if the question is asked immediately after a class has finished and another class is coming into the ring. I'm afraid that unless something is obviously wrong with the dog my answer is, 'Not much, but there were others I liked better'.

Chapter 4

OTHER ACTIVITIES

Racing is a popular 'other activity' at lurcher shows. I've never followed it myself mainly because the few times I did put any of my dogs in for a race they soon realised that they were chasing a bundle of rags and lost interest, but there is no doubt that a great many people enjoy it. Some only attend shows for the racing.

In the early days of lurcher shows the racing tended to be haphazard and a great many dogs were damaged as a result: from fighting, from badly layed out tracks – in particular, no protection for the towing mechanism with the result that dogs ran into whatever machinery there was – and from dogs let loose from the side of the track while a race was in progress.

For a long time many shows held out against using muzzles for racing; it spoilt the 'macho' image of the owners. Their dogs were not going to be stopped from having a fight if they wanted one. Sadly, the same attitude persists here and there in the lurcher – and terrier – world: 'I'm a hard man, my dog will take any punishment' is their outlook but thankfully more and more shows are coming round to the necessity of using muzzles; one Club that insisted on it from the start is the Sussex Longdogs Association who have always run their racing very efficiently. What more stupid and unnecessary way is there of having one's dog torn and bitten than by putting it in for a race without all dogs wearing muzzles?

The race track should be long enough; there is little point in racing dogs for less than 300 yards and a quarter of a mile is better still; and races should be for dogs of approximately equal size. Lurchers of all sorts, and particularly those that have a large proportion of greyhound in them, will go for anything galloping in front of them. They mean no harm, and are very sorry afterwards, but a whippet or small lurcher that has been savaged by a larger dog coming up from behind will always be looking round in anticipation of trouble.

Whether straight tracks or curved are used partly depends on the ground and the equipment available. At the early shows held at Upper Lambourn the race track was horseshoe shaped, the inner 'rail' formed of netting. This provided exciting racing, though memory suggests that the curve was fairly sharp as many dogs ran very wide when the lure jerked outwards. When the show moved to Seven Barrows a curved track was again laid out, this time the inner

45

rail being made of electric sheep netting. Slower dogs, and those that were left at the start, soon realised that by cutting the corner they could catch up on the lure and many did just that; they jumped over the netting and galloped across to join in the race again near the finish, something that I do not remember seeing at the old site. Lurchers are not fools. If a curved track is to be used the inner fence should be formed of something high enough to deter would-be corner cutters. Whippet Racing Clubs who use horseshoe or circular tracks use netting but whippets are much smaller dogs and those that do race are trained to following the lure. Many large lurchers, shown a lure for the first time, will go the shortest way to catch it.

Some dogs particularly puppies, are so intent on catching the lure that they crash into the straw bales protecting the towing mechanism. This can be avoided by putting the machine and batteries ten or twenty yards off the line of the lure with a pulley, protected by a straw bale, just beyond the winning post. If the lure turns at an angle of about 30 degrees it will be enough to allow dogs to gallop on beyond the turn without damaging themselves. By the time they realise that the lure has gone sideways it can be safely hidden under a sack.

I believe that Tony Mills was the first person to organise 'speed jumping', at Holkham in 1979. He laid out a straight track between walls of straw bales, five bales high, with half a dozen jumps made of straw bales, four bales high. The dog was handed over to a 'slipper' and the owner ran to the far end where he stood on a platform of straw bales so that his dog could see him. There he whistled or called and his dog ran up to him, jumping the piles of bales, against a stop watch.

Tony Mills' original idea has been copied at many shows, usually successfully where the owner has had to go the far end of the course and call or whistle up his dog; unsuccessfully where the owner has merely been required to run alongside his dog encouraging it over the jumps. Speed jumping should test the dog's speed, not its owner's.

I copied the idea in 1979 at the North Bucks Show at Stowe but I used more orthodox fences; three lots of sheep hurdles, a straw bale wall, a bush fence and a farm gate. However, I made two mistakes. I laid out the course – or jumping lane, to use the old cavalry term – on slightly convex ground which meant that only the largest dogs could see their owners at the far end of the course, even though they were standing on a pile of straw bales; and I placed the split chestnut paling, used as rails for the course and, incidentally, borrowed from the local Council, up against the fences which meant that the spectators could, and did, interfere with the dogs. I remember amongst others an old acquaintance, Brandon Cadbury, encouraging a reluctant jumper with his golf umbrella. The following year I moved the course to an old, shallow quarry. Using this bowl-shaped ground meant that the smallest dog could see its owner over the fences and the spectators were kept back round the edge of the bowl by ropes, incidentally giving them a much better view of the whole action. Speed jumping should not be confined to lurchers. The fat Labrador following its sometimes

equally fat owner down the jumping lane will give the spectators more enter-
tainment than the fastest jumping lurcher. But for less athletic dogs there must
be a gap in the side fence somewhere around the middle of the course so that
those that can get no further may be extracted without too much loss of time.
It merely means angling out a section of fencing but the gap should be pointing
backwards so that dogs cannot see it unless they turn around towards the start.
On the same principle there should be a small hole under each solid fence so
that small dogs and terriers can go under what they cannot jump; a nine inch
drain pipe will do well for this. They can go under hurdles and gates easily but
if any solid fences are used – such as straw bale walls, etc – the holes should
alternate from left to right from fence to fence so that it is not too easy for them.
At the 1981 North Bucks Show the fastest time of all was achieved by Coursing
Supporters Club Anne Mackenzie's tiny terrier *Spice*, who ran twice down the
course to find out where the drain pipes were and on its third attempt produced
a winning time of one second better than the fastest lurcher. Some objections
were made but there was nothing in the schedule to say that dogs had to go
over, and not under, each fence.

At Stowe we used a narrow 'chute' to lead dogs and owners to the start.
This did save barging and shoving and it meant that the brave person acting
as slipper did not have a crowd of people and dogs round him. When I have
been organising speed jumping I have always offered the slipper a pair of thick
leather hedging gloves because many dogs get excited by their owners calling
them from the far end of the course and some of them, mostly non-lurchers,
can snatch and bite in their efforts to get away.

Lure chasing is an effort to simulate coursing by running the towing wire of a
lure round pullies, thus trying to reproducing the turns that a live hare makes
when coursed. It is, in fact, two dogs racing after a lure which suddenly jerks
to left or right as the string goes round a pulley though the sharp turn of the
hare is not copied because the lure swings wide before taking up its new line
and the dogs do not turn as sharply as they would in natural coursing.

There is certainly no objection to lure chasing for those who enjoy it when
it takes place in a large enough area to make it realistic, and by large enough I
mean at least a ten or twelve acre field. I saw this done by the National Lurcher
Racing Club as part of their Field Trial Day near Coventry, in 1984. As *Lure
Chasing* it was efficiently run in a field that must have been at least 20 acres.
From memory there were three turning points for the lure but instead of pulleys
on spindles, stuck into the ground, on which there must, in the end, be a chance
of dog laming itself, three people held metal rings through which the lure string
passed. As the lure approached the first man he let go of the ring and the lure
jerked off towards the next ring holder; the other two men did the same, the
lure ending up at the towing machine with the three rings collected up next to
it on the string. The great advantage of this method was that each 'course' could
take a different line by the ring holders altering their positions on the field; dogs
running a second time found the lure changing direction at different places to

their first run. Another advantage seemed to be that instead of the person towing the lure out again to the start having to run it round three pulleys, the three ring holders merely walked to the middle of the field, each picked up a ring as the tower passed him and then returned towards the hedge.

But it is a great mistake to put on *lure chasing* ('simulated coursing') in a show or country fair arena which will not be more than one acre or two in size, with a slipper in a red coat, dogs in coloured collars and someone with equivalent coloured flags to show the 'winner' of each 'course' and then to tell the spectators that proper coursing is like the shambles that they are watching. I say shambles because in such a small space the dogs are hardly into their stride before the lure reaches the first pulley, they swing wide at each turn as the lure swings wide, there will certainly not be room to use more than two pulleys, when the lure disappears by the towing mechanism the two dogs are not yet out of breath and they career round the ring looking for something else to chase. If it is being run as a knockout competition, as in real coursing, the dogs in the second and subsequent rounds know where the lure will turn and cut corners accordingly. The 'judging' can only be guesswork at the best.

I have several objections to this sort of activity being called *coursing*. In coursing the dogs usually dictate when the hare turns. A hare escaping from any predator will run in a more or less straight line for whatever refuge it has in mind, perhaps a wood. When a greyhound – or lurcher or whippet, etc. – is close enough to try and snatch the hare, the hare will turn away from that dog, i.e., if the dog is coming up on the hare's right hand side the hare will turn to the left; the dog is prepared for this and will turn after the hare as sharply as it can. Many whippets will turn with the hare and hardly lose any ground at all; the hare almost never turns unexpectedly. When a dog is chasing a lure it does not know where the turning pulleys are and the turns will therefore be unexpected; as a result the dog will run wide and will take some distance to get back onto the line of the lure. If an event such as this is run in the arena of a show, or 'country fair' the turning pulleys have to be fairly near the ringside; there is never room enough to put them anywhere else. With dogs running wide at every turn, sooner or later a dog will crash into a wooden post or some other obstacle at the ringside – a push chair full of child, perhaps? – and more or less damage will be done, certainly to the dog and most probably to one or more spectators. A 60lb dog travelling at 25mph (it would not be doing much more in a small ring) can break a man's knee when the collision is unexpected. *This is not coursing and the spectators should not be told that it is, or that it even resembles coursing.*

Another objection to simulated coursing is that it is just what the antis want coursing people to do and it *can* be used for the wrong sort of publicity. Finally, where it is organised in public, at a show of some sort, as a knockout competition, the owners paying to run their dogs (I have heard of an entry fee of as much as £5 per dog), 'judging' this sort of thing cannot possibly be done by any combination of the rules of coursing. No system of points can be laid down and the judge's opinion can be challenged without either side being able to produce 'proof' of their point of view. With, say, a 16 dog knockout stake at £5, there is £80 at stake, let alone anything that the show organisers may add and I would not like to be the judge who has to justify his opinion under such circumstances.

It is astonishing to see the height that some lurchers will jump, or at least the height of solid fence that they will scramble over. I think that the highest I have seen is 8 feet 9 inches but no doubt there have been higher jumps made. For a 24 inch dog, an 8 foot wooden wall must seem enormous but I suppose that a horse, faced with the stone wall at Dublin or the wall at Olympia, or Earls Court, must be equally brave. There is no doubt about the popularity to spectators of high-jumping at lurcher shows but I do feel that some sort of raised, soft landing should be provided – two or three layers of straw bales, perhaps, to lessen the shock to dogs' front legs and shoulders.

Show jumping was run at the early – and later – 'Lambourns', based on horse show jumping and using the same fences, and it has been copied at many shows; owners running alongside their dogs which might or might not be on leads. Other than the dog jumping where it is told to jump it is more a test of the owner's running ability than the dog's.

Obstacle racing, too, was run at the early 'Lambourns' but I have very seldom seen an equivalent since then. The course included scrambling through motor tyres, over and under rails and under a pig net – or was it a tarpaulin? – and finishing with a sack race, the owners having to remain fastened to their dogs throughout. It was a popular item, particularly with children, and produced a lot of laughs. Some present day organisers could well think about introducing such an item to lessen the seriousness that affects many lurcher shows.

All lurchers should of course be obedient up to a point but if obedience tests are to be properly run they do take time. Relatively few dogs can be put through a sensible test in the time available. At Upper Lambourn the test included dogs being wheeled in wheelbarrows – most of them baled out after a yard or two – and when dogs were told to lie down and the owners walked away for five yards or so a saucer of cooked bacon rinds was placed in front of each dog while the owners ordered 'NO'. Some dogs scoffed the bacon rinds straight away, others drooled and crawled closer to the saucer and few abstained; those that did looked beseechingly at Master. At the first show of all the test was won by a 'mongrel' and at the second, or perhaps the third show, it was won by a pure bred whippet. It was not meant to be a serious test but those early shows were not meant to be taken seriously and were all the more fun for that reason.

I think that the first serious obedience test I saw was at the Croome and West Warwickshire HSC Show at Wootton Wawen in about 1977; I cannot find a record of the date. It was a well run and well thought out test, taking owner and dog over hedges, through railings, in and out of a small spinney and finishing with a 'hare' being pulled past the sitting dog which had to remain still until told to 'Go'. From memory, the test took at least seven minutes per dog or perhaps more, and at the end of the day there was still a queue waiting to take part.

49

An ambitious day's testing was run by the National Lurcher Racing Club near Coventry in 1984. The tests, spread over four or five fields, started with each dog being sent over a plain wire fence. Most jumped, but the fence was not very wide and some went round. For the next test, owner and dog walked along the side of a field and a lure suddenly appeared out of the hedge, going diagonally across to the next hedge; dogs that chased without being told to do so were penalised. In the next field dogs were tested for their reactions to ferrets and then shown three drain pipes, buried in the turf with open ends, in one of which was a rabbit, a necessarily dead one; dogs had to indicate which drain held the rabbit and the first dog tested showed what he thought by cocking his leg on the correct drain. For the fifth test owner and dog stood some yards from another drainpipe buried in the turf; a lure suddenly appeared out of the drainpipe and was towed across to the nearest hedge, the dog not to move until told to do so. One dog to fail this test was a very powerful smooth fawn bitch who moved so fast, without orders, that she had the lure before it had gone five yards; she came low down in the final placings but that was the one which I would have taken home – I've never seen such quick reactions. The sixth test was for the dog to sit behind a hedge while master walked away, dog not to move until called. Surprisingly, many competitors failed this test. The seventh test consisted of each owner in turn sending his dog out to 'quarter' a somewhat tussocky grass field. A lure had been placed behind a tussock and was pulled when the dog got near. It was a good test in theory but it was obvious that not all the competitors knew how to work a field and they did not go far from master. I think that a eighth test, in yet another field, consisted of a simple retrieve of a thrown dummy. After a lunch break dogs were tested in 'simulated coursing'. It was well run and I refer to it under its own heading but I thought that it was a pity to waste time with it after so much trouble had been taken over setting up the morning's tests. Whilst it gave the dogs a gallop it was not an obedience test and without the 'simulated coursing' more than the dozen dogs could have been put through the seven or eight tests.

It was an interesting attempt to tests dogs' obedience under field conditions but I did not think that it quite came off. Lurchers do not have to show the almost unthinking obedience of Kennel Club obedience tests; basic walking to heel, sitting and staying, retrieving a thrown dummy, etc, can be tested in quite a small area and a reasonable number put through in the time available so long as too much paper work is not done.

In the past when faced with two dogs between which I could not make up my mind I have, on occasions, asked the owners to take off collars and leads and walk on with dogs at heel. This is usually enough to show which dog is obedient and that is the lurcher that should get the prize. If there is a fence or railings or a wall nearby one can ask the owners to send their dogs over and call them straight back

The now defunct Thames Valley Lurcher Association ran comprehensive tests at their shows and Tony Diprose and Dennis Eastwood carry on the good work at their shows at Newbury and elsewhere. Indeed, many shows do run tests, some more successful than others. An alternative to a formal test and one in which many more dogs can take part, is the Working Companion Class or 'Poachers Dog' Class. Dogs are off leads and having walked round the ring a couple of times owners can be asked to perform various manoeuvres such as walking across the ring and dropping their dog halfway, dropping the dog and picking it up again when walking past, etc. Any such class is worthwhile even if only to show spectators that lurchers are not all undisciplined tearaways. If a short demonstration of lurcher obedience can be put on in the main ring of a country fair it is well worth doing.

PART II
LONGDOGS AT WORK

Chapter 5

COURSING

THE HARE, THE QUARRY

The Brown Hare, Lepus capensis, has one of the largest ranges of any land mammal, inhabiting the temperate lowlands and savannas from Europe to China and it may have preceded early man onto English soil. The Mountain Hare, Lepus timidus, had reached Ireland before Ireland was cut off from England by the sea but the Brown Hare is not native to Ireland. When the last Great Ice Age retreated northwards England was for a time still connected to the Continent by a land bridge and it was across this bridge that many species of plants and animals followed the ice northwards, amongst them the Brown Hare. Then came early man, man the hunter then man the agriculturalist and now man the destroyer of the countryside.

For many thousands of years the Brown Hare has lived and thrived in the English countryside despite being the prime supper of predators from man to feral cat. The hare is born in the open, lives all its life in the open and dies in the open. It does not escape by flying or by going to ground – or very seldom. It can and does swim on occasions. It has so far survived in the open because of its ability to lie still, half hidden in its form, and by its instant reaction to danger, being able to jump from stillness to full gallop in two strides. Once galloping the hare can stop and turn about in its own length and continue galloping and turning until it either tires out its pursuers or is caught; and if hares were easily caught they would have died out by now. Escape is a daily occupation. Some believe that hare numbers increase and decrease in cycles but until the 1940's the hare population was so big – on land which suited hares – that many estates finished each shooting season with hare shoots; in some areas such as East Anglia the bag would be counted in thousands rather than hundreds. Now, whilst hares are by no means rare or in any danger of dying out as some conservationists would have us believe they have become locally scarce except where they are not disturbed and on those estates and farms where organised coursing takes place and where hares are preserved and the ground strongly keepered. Many factors have brought about the reduction of the hare population; changes in farming practices, vast increases in the use of chemical sprays, the enormous spread of bricks and concrete, tarmac and cars are some of them and, in general, the post-War change from mixed farming to agri-business with its plains of single crops.

A further factor in the decline of the hare population from its very high numbers is the increase in the fox population. Hares form a large part of the fox's diet in the summer and autumn when leverets are caught in their forms and when corn crops and other vegetation make escape more difficult than in winter when the fields are relatively bare. The increase in the fox population is partly due to the increasing areas where packs of hounds can no longer hunt; motorways, A roads and urban and suburban spread sterilise land for hunting and there are many acres of countryside which are no longer 'keepered so foxes are not controlled as they once were. I mention this subject again in Chapter 6.

Hares are nocturnal and they have three requirements in order to flourish: cover by day, mixed vegetation to eat and freedom from constant disturbance. The cover by day may vary from small woods and spinneys, hedgerows and root crops to old, weathered ploughing, something that is seldom seen nowadays. As soon as a crop is harvested the stubble is removed by one means or another – thankfully burning is beginning to lose its appeal – the cultivators are into the fields, the next crop is sown and the land is left flat and bare with no cover for hares or grass and weeds to eat. A relative late-comer to to the list of enemies of the hare is the slug pellet, now needed in ever increasing doses to combat slugs which eat the ever increasing sowings of oil seed rape.

Those who wish to see coursing stopped make much propaganda out of hares being killed; this matter should be looked at in perspective. Hares are coursed on their own ground, almost always where they have been born and certainly where they know every field and hedge and gap; under N.C.C. Rules coursing may not take place on ground into which hares have been introduced in the previous three months or where they are not at complete liberty. The length of the slip takes away some of the advantage of the greyhound's superior speed; about 3 hares in 10 are killed quickly and the rest escape unwounded. At hare shoots, where hares are numerous, by no means every hare is killed cleanly; many escaped to die of wounds and gangrene. I do not know of any statistics showing the number of hares killed on the roads every year.

About 600 hares are killed each season at organised coursing meetings run under rules. More are killed by private coursing and un-organised coursing but they too are killed quickly and there are no wounded hares left to die later. In contrast, the number of farm animals sent for slaughter for human, and other consumption was 69,500 cattle, 351,000 sheep and 287,500 pigs *in one week* in March, 1989.

THE RULES OF ORGANISED COURSING

There are two sorts of coursing, private coursing and public coursing. Private coursing has been in existence ever since man moved out of the trees and walked on two legs with a dog beside him. For thousands of years coursing was a method of killing game for food. The game varied from deer to rabbits, from large to small, and the dogs used varied with the game; the same natural divisions still occur, sometimes legally sometimes illegally.

As the early tribes of men spread from the Middle East so they took their dogs with them, the dogs developing in different ways in different countries according to the climate, the ground and what they hunted. So long as hunting for food was the main purpose men used spears and bows and arrows and dogs were for finding, chasing and holding where game was not initially killed. As 'civilisation' spread so food sources increased until wild game became a necessity only to those without access to farmed animals. Hunting, from being a necessity became a sport for the high and mighty who took care that those not so privileged did not share in it other than as helpers. This was done, in England, by restricting the ownership of lands where hunting took place and restricting the ownership of the dogs used, the longdogs, the greyhounds. I have touched on this subject in *Lurchers and Longdogs* and in *The Poacher's Companion*.

Gradually those who used greyhounds for private coursing for sport, either on their own or on neighbours' land, felt the urge to try their dogs against other people's dogs. So public coursing started. Although Rules had been drawn up in the 16th Century one does not know how widely they were known and there must have been innumerable arguments over which was the better dog; which dog had won the course? What was the criterion? Was it the dog which killed the hare? Five hundred years ago this probably was the deciding factor; many present-day lurcher owners would agree. But remembering that the greyhound owners were the landowners, educated men many of them, they would have had Latin and Greek beaten into them at whatever academies they attended and many of them would have agreed with the Ancients that:

> The true sportsman does not take out his dogs to destroy the Hares, but for the sake of the course, and the contest between the dogs and the Hares, and is glad if the Hare escapes.

This is still true of the public coursing man and many private coursers today, a fact not understood by those against field sports.

Gradually, over many years and with much argument, the rules of coursing evolved. If one has time to spare – and time is needed as well as a basic knowledge of coursing – it is interesting to work one's way through Thomas Thacker's reasonings on the subject (*The Courser's Companion*, 1823) but it is academic coursing history now. The Rules drawn up by the newly-formed National Coursing Club in 1857 are, with amendments found necessary through the years, the Rules of the National Coursing Club today. These Rules govern all public coursing with greyhounds in England, Scotland and Wales as well as, with certain adaptions, coursing with pure-bred whippets, salukis and deer-hounds. To understand coursing it is necessary to understand the rules and how they are applied; without knowing the rules coursing is incomprehensible and it is almost the only sport to which this applies (I use 'sport' in its true sense as opposed to 'games').

Whilst the rules of coursing have been explained many times over many years (I have added my small quota, broadly in *Lurchers and Longdogs* and in detail in *The English Whippet*), a certain amount of experience in watching coursing as well as reading is needed to understand them. I have found otherwise experienced lurcher people say such things as, 'You let the hares out of boxes, don't you?' (I took that person to a proper coursing meeting where she was interested to see what really went on). Rules dealing with administration, organisation, membership etc., etc., are straight forward; it is the rules governing some of the conduct of meetings and, above all, judging, which newcomers find difficult. I have therefore tried to illustrate some of these rules, at least those which can be illustrated, in the hope that pictures may explain that which can be obscure in writing.

Coursing in the dictionary meaning is 'the sport of chasing hares or other game with greyhounds by sight'. By common usage it came to mean coursing under rules. If one spoke of 'a coursing man' one meant someone who took part in meetings under National Coursing Club Rules and, latterly, under the same rules amended for whippets, salukis and deerhounds. The essence of those rules is:

> The dog which scores most points during the continuance of the course is to be declared the winner. The principle is to be carried out by estimating the value of the work done by each dog, as seen by the Judge . . .

The *Points of the Course* are laid down for speed, the go-bye, the turn, the wrench, the kill and the trip. It is all very formal and to the uninitiated, seeing such coursing for the first time, makes little sense. Whilst there is nothing in the rule book that says specifically that the dog which cuts a corner and does not follow the hare's track will be penalised this does happen in practice and moreover, a dog can lose a course by killing too soon if his opponent is ahead on points. Points can be worked off but a kill only rates one point at the most. For instance, red collar is 3 points in the lead and white collar gets in, turns the hare and then kills. White collar will at the most get one point for the turn and another point for the kill leaving red collar still one point in the lead and the winner of the course. At the opposite end of coursing the purpose of the lurcher is to 'Hunt, jump, catch, kill and carry' and the sooner he kills the sooner he will get his tongue back in and be ready for the next run. He should not waste time totting up points.

EXTRACTS FROM THE RULES OF THE NATIONAL COURSING CLUB

18. TAKING DOGS TO SLIPS
(1) Every dog must be brought to slips in its proper turn without delay, under a penalty (£5). If absent for more than ten minutes (after being called by the Slip Steward or his assistant), its opponent shall be entitled to claim the course, subject to the discretion of the Stewards, and shall in that case run a bye. If

both dogs are absent then both dogs shall be disqualified.

(2) No dog shall be put into slips until thirty minutes after its course in the previous round, without the consent of the nominator and permission of the Stewards. The time to count from the time the Judge signalled the result of that course.

(3) The owner and trainer are jointly answerable for a dog being put into slips at the right time and on the right side and in the right collar, under a penalty (£10).

(4) Every dog brought to slips shall wear a collar not less than two inches wide, and coloured red for the dog on the left hand side and white for the dog on the right hand side of the slips. The upper dog on the card shall be placed on the left hand side in the slips and the lower dog on the right hand side.

Coursing is run on the knock-out principle, dogs being numbered down the card in each stake and the winner of each pair running against the winner of the pair below in each round. Stakes are normally run in multiples of 8, i.e., 8 dogs, 16 dogs, 32 dogs or 64 dogs. Arbitrary placing in slips according to the original draw makes it a matter of luck whether a dog is favoured by the ground or the run of hares.

19. CONTROL OF DOGS

(1) The control of all matters connected with slipping dogs, or permitting them to be placed in slips, shall rest with the Stewards.

(2) An owner, nominator, trainer or assistant, after putting his dog in the slips may go forward to catch it on the same side as his dog is in the slips, or on the same side as his/her opponent if they so agree, so that no inconvenience is caused to the Slipper and so that there is no interference with the dogs or line of run of the hare. No person shall halloa the dogs on while running. The Stewards may impose a fine (not exceeding £10) on any person infringing this Rule.

(3) Any dog found to be beyond control in the slips may, by order of the Stewards, be taken out of the slips and disqualified.

(4) No other person than the Slipper shall be in the shy except with the permission of the Stewards, and neither shall dogs be in the shy other than those in the charge of the Slipper.

The 'shy' is the screen behind which the Slipper stands with the two dogs, to hide them from hares coming through the hedge from behind. It can vary from an actual screen of wood or canvas or wattle hurdles to a pile of straw bales or even a Land Rover. Once a hare has decided to go through a hedge it will run on up the next field unless some person or dog turns it back as it emerges and even then it is more likely to run sideways along the hedge than go back through again. Fit greyhounds weighing upwards of 70lbs each can take some controlling, specially if hares come through past the shy in pairs, when the Slipper cannot let the dogs go, or too far away for the dogs to be slipped. The

Slipper therefore loops the slack of the slip lead – which is about 6 foot long – round the two dogs to hold them together.

20. THE SLIP

(1) **The slip shall be made at the sole discretion of the Slipper. The length of slip must necessarily vary with the nature of the ground and should not be less than 80 yards. The Slipper shall not slip the dogs if in his opinion the hare is in a weak condition or 'balled-up'.**

(2) **No dog shall be hand-slipped without the permission of the Stewards.**

(3) **If one dog gets out of the slips, the Slipper shall let the other dog go immediately, the Judge to decide the course as set out in Rule 25 (1) (a).**

(4) **Once the dogs are slipped they shall not be touched or handled by their owner or trainer or any other person until the Judge has given his decision, except in a case where a dog has suffered severe injury and is unable to continue the course, such an injury to be verified by a Veterinary Surgeon on the field, or the Stewards of the meeting. Infringement of this Rule shall result in the disqualification of the dog concerned in the stake being run.**

Under normal conditions, with efficient beating and flanking on the 'beat' side of the shy and flanking on the running ground, hares will run straight past the shy and up the running ground at about three-quarter speed. This gives the Slipper some 15 seconds, from the time he first sees the hare, to decide if the hare is fully grown, is sound, looks fit and its feet are not clogged up with mud. In these fifteen seconds he has to make up his mind to slip, get both dogs looking at the hare, get them balanced together and pulling at the end of the slips, run forward to get the dogs moving and slip them when the hare reaches a pre-determined spot some 80 to 120 yards up the running ground, depending on circumstances. With whippets and their shorter slip, the Slipper has five seconds to make the same decisions. I remember Lilah Shennan once saying that whilst a Judge can make some bad decisions a bad Slipper, or one off form, can ruin a whole meeting.

I have said 'with efficient beating and flanking'; driving hares for coursing is a skilled business and one that is not usually understood by gamekeepers who have not been coursing before. When driving game, be it partridges, pheasants or hares, to a line of guns the 'keeper is moving the game forward on a front that is measured by the number of guns. So whilst the 'hot seat' is usually in the centre of the line it does not really matter whether the bulk of the game goes right, left or centre so long as it goes forward. When driving hares for coursing the 'keeper should imagine that he is driving them, one at a time, to one person using a muzzle loader with a limited range and which takes five minutes to re-load. The slipping distance is 80 yards or more but the 80 yards should be measured straight forward from the shy so the nearer to the shy that hares come through from the beat the easier it is for the slipper. If a hare comes through from the beat 80 yards to his right or left it may be out of slipping distance; if it does edge in to his front the slip may well favour the dog on whose side the hare is running. This is where the placing of the flanking beaters is so important. If the two or three men on either side are too far apart hares will come through from the beat too far away from the slipper. When the beat starts it should be shaped like a horseshoe, the heels of which are closer together than the middle.

2. ORGANISATION OF COURSING MEETINGS

(7) The Committee shall appoint (and shall notify the Stewards of such appointment) four 'Pickers-up' who throughout the coursing meeting shall be stationed two on each side of the coursing ground and as near as is practicable to where the courses are likely to end. If the hare be brought down Pickers-up shall without delay go to the hare and satisfy themselves that it is dead, and if it is not dead they shall kill it forthwith.

21. DUTY TO DISPATCH THE HARE

Notwithstanding that this Code of Rules provides for the appointment of four 'Pickers-up' ar every Coursing Meeting it shall be the duty of any person (including any person who has gone forward in accordance with Rule 19 (2) but excluding the Judge) who is in the vicinity of any hare brought down, before taking any other action, to satisfy himself that the hare is dead and if it is not dead to kill it forthwith.

22. DECISION OF THE JUDGE

(2) He shall on the termination of each course, immediately deliver his decision, either by displaying a red or white handkerchief corresponding to the collar of the winner, or when the colours of the dogs are more distinguishable than their collars, he may call the colour of the winning dog aloud.

(3) He shall not recall or reverse his decision, on any pretext whatever, after it has been declared; but no decision shall be delivered until the Judge is perfectly satisfied that the course is absolutely terminated.

The Judge holds out – or should hold out – the coloured handkerchief in the appropriate hand, i.e., RED in his left hand, since red collar goes into slips on the left and WHITE in his right hand since white collar goes into slips on the right. This is not only logical, but as the Judge may be quite a long way from the Flag Steward and spectators when he gives his decision it is often easier to distinguish the hand that is held out than the colour of the 'flag', particularly white against the sky.

The reason for dogs wearing coloured collars is that when two fawns, or red fawns or blacks are running against each other there may be no other way of distinguishing between them at a distance than by coloured collars. This rule came into being about 100 years ago but collars were being worn some time before that.

23. PRINCIPLES OF JUDGING

The Judge shall decide all courses on the one uniform principle that the dog which scores the greater number of points during the continuance of the course is to be declared the winner. The principle is to be carried out by estimating the value of the work done by each dog, **AS SEEN BY THE JUDGE**, upon a balance of points according to the scale hereafter laid down, from which also are to be deducted certain specified allowances and penalties.

This is the Rule that decides which dog wins. The Judge is mounted so that he, or she, can ride as near as possible at right angles to the run of the hare and dogs; only being in this position can he see which dog is leading and by how much. I have put 'as seen by the Judge' in capital letters because what the Judge sees from on horseback can be very different from the view of the spectators – including owners and trainers of dogs – from where they are standing.

Whilst the Judge should ride as near at a right angle to the run of hare and dogs he should never be so close as to impede or influence their run, particularly that of the hare, nor should he at any time get between the hare and her probable escape. It can happen that hare and dogs come very close to the Judge at which point he should stand very still or he may ride over one or the other.

The Judge faces certain problems, even at a driven meeting, one being the swinging hare, the hare which comes through wide of the shy on the side on which he is standing and turns away from him; with this course the Judge only sees the two dogs from behind until he manages to gallop up to his proper place at right-angles to them. Worst of all from the Judge's point of view is the walked meeting, or walked course – usually only encountered with greyhounds when a field is being cleared before the beat starts, – when a hare gets up on the opposite side of the walking line from where the Judge is riding. Unless he is on a very fast and handy horse he is unlikely to get level with where the dogs are running until they have turned the hare at least once; he therefore has to judge the 'lead' from behind the two dogs which is an almost impossible task, as anyone who has stood in the shy and watched courses from that point of view will confirm.

24. POINTS OF THE COURSE

(1) The points of the course are:

(a) SPEED – which shall be estimated as one, two or three points according to the degree of superiority shown.

(b) The GO-BYE – two points or, if gained on the outer circle, three points.

(c) The TURN – one point.

(d) The WRENCH – half a point.

(e) The KILL – not more than one point, in proportion to the degree of merit displayed in that kill, which may be of no value.

(f) The TRIP – one point.

24. POINTS OF THE COURSE (continued)

(2) In estimating the value of speed to the hare the Judge must take into account the several forms in which it may be displayed:

(a) Where in the run-up a clear lead is gained by one of the dogs, in which case one, two or three points may be given, according to the length of lead, apart from a turn or a wrench. In awarding these points the Judge shall take into consideration the merit of a lead obtained by a dog which has lost ground from the start, either from being unsighted or which has to run the outer circle.

(b) Where one dog leads so long as the hare runs straight but loses the lead from her bending round decidedly in favour of the slower dog of her own accord, in which case the dog shall score one point for the speed shown, and the other dog score one point for the first turn, but under no circumstances is speed without subsequent work to be allowed to decide a course.

(3) If a dog, after gaining the first six points, still keeps possession of the hare by superior speed, he shall have double the proscribed allowance for the subsequent points made before his opponent begins to score.

The Rules do not say that so many points should be given for a lead to the hare of so many lengths so a three or more lengths lead is not automatically given three points. Individual Judges have their own methods of assessing a lead but the important words are 'the merit of a lead'. If two brilliant dogs are running together the Judge may well look on a one length lead as more meritorious than a five lengths lead between two mediocre dogs.

24. POINTS OF THE COURSE (continued)
(4)

(a) The GO-BYE – Two points or if gained on the outer circle three points. The GO-BYE is where a dog starts a clear length behind his opponent and yet passes him in a straight run and gets a clear length before him.

This is probably the least seen manoeuvre; for it to happen one dog must be appreciably faster than the other. Once a dog tires it may well be that his opponent, being fitter, gives him several go-byes but by that time it is unlikely that either dog is still scoring. In any case it is not always easy to confirm that the faster dog 'starts a length behind his opponent and finishes a length in front'. The late Jack Chadwick used to say that spectators saw more go-byes than he did when he was judging.

24. POINTS OF THE COURSE **(continued)**
(4)

(b) The TURN – One point. The TURN is where the hare is brought round at not less than a right angle from her previous line.

The Judge, being close to the dogs and hare, is in a better position than spectators to decide what angle the hare has turned. More turns are seen early in a course than later when the dogs are not pressing the hare so much.

24. POINTS OF THE COURSE **(continued)**
(4)

(c) The WRENCH – half a point. The WRENCH is where the hare is bent from her line at less than a right-angle; but where she only leaves her line to suit herself, and not from the dog pressing her, nothing is to be allowed.

The difference between a TURN and a WRENCH is a matter of degrees and the Judge has to rely on his experience in deciding which is which and allotting points. True turns happen more frequently early in a course and tend to become wrenches when the dogs are losing their speed. Once this happens and the hare is galloping on towards whatever cover she is making for she will often bear from side to side making it look, from a distance, as if the leading dog is scoring. Often only the Judge and perhaps pickers-up and far flankers are close enough to see that the hare is 'suiting herself' and is not being pressed to turn. It may well be that with her eyes set high on her head she finds it easier to keep the following dogs in view by bending left and right.

24. POINTS OF THE COURSE (continued)
(4)

(d) **The KILL** – Not more than one point, in proportion to the degree of merit displayed in that kill, which may be of no value. The merit of a KILL must be estimated according to whether a dog by his own superior dash and skill, bears the hare; whether he picks her up by any little accidental circumstances favouring him, or whether she is turned into his mouth, as it were, by the other dog.

Killing hares is what the opponents of coursing make most noise about but in fact, over the seasons the proportion of kills at meetings is about 30 per cent of hares coursed, 3 in 10. The brilliant dog which races up to the hare and seizes it in full gallop will probably get a full point added to whatever he has got for the lead up. Where the two dogs catch the hare at the end of a muddling course the actual killer may get no points at all and a dog can kill too soon to lose a course, as I have explained.

24. POINTS OF THE COURSE (continued)
(4)

(e) **The TRIP** – One point. The TRIP, or unsuccessful effort to kill, is where the hare is thrown off her legs, or where the dog flecks her but cannot hold her.

Unless there is something physically wrong with her a hare that is flecked is almost never touched by the dogs again and almost always makes her escape. The hare in the illustration picked herself up and escaped under a wire fence behind the photographer.

25. ALLOWANCES FOR ACCIDENTS
The following allowances shall be made for accidents to a dog during a course; but in every case they shall only be deducted from the other dog's score:

(a) After a fair slip no allowance shall be made for a dog being unsighted, but the Judge may decide the course or declare the course to be undecided or no-course as he thinks fit.

(b) Where a hare bears very decidedly in favour of one of the dogs after the first or subsequent turns, in which case the next point shall not be scored by the dog unduly favoured, or only half his points allowed according to circumstances.

(c) No dog shall receive any allowance for a fall or an accident, with the exception of when pressing his hare, in which case his opponent shall not count the next point made.

If on the run-up one dog is unsighted and runs off at a tangent, the dog that is coursing the hare does not score until either the other dog re-joins the course or he turns the hare for the first time. The run-up is a test of speed, a dog on its own is not being tested and no points can be given.

27. SECOND HARE

If a second hare be started during a course and one of the dogs follow her, the course shall end there. If the points at this stage be equal, the dog that continues to course the original hare shall be awarded the course.

'Second hare' can come under the same heading as 'unsighted' since both can occur because of dead ground but both do, many times, occur because of the in-bred tendency of the greyhound to chase anything that moves. The galloping dog, with its head alternating between 20 and 24 inches from the ground at each stride, starts after the hare which it saw coming past the shy and going on up the running ground. The running ground may be flat green turf but apart from any undulations of the ground it may equally be dead grass – 'fog' to use an old name – and tussocks, yellowy-brown in colour, through which a galloping hare may well be invisible part of the time so it is not all that surprising that greyhounds do occasionally lose sight of the hare they started to course.

28. DOGS GETTING LOOSE

(1) Any person allowing a dog or dogs to get loose during a meeting may, at the discretion of the Stewards, be fined a sum not exceeding £10 for each loose dog.

(2) If the loose dog join in the course which is being run and is owned or part-owned by the Nominator or Joint-Nominator of one of the dogs engaged therein, the other dog shall be deemed the winner unless such Nominator or Joint-Nominator can satisfy the Stewards that it had not been possible to get the loose dog taken up after running its own course.

(3) The course is not to be considered as necessarily ended when a third dog joins in.

At some clubs where many of the running grounds are bounded by walls or dykes it is not always easy to stop greyhounds pursuing hares into the far distance; many times one has seen owners, trainers or handlers setting out to try and collect a dog that has followed its hare over the wall surrounding the running ground and out into the country. If hares are coming through from the beat the Slipper cannot wait until every dog is picked up and it does happen that a dog returning from a course, tired through he may be, will join in a course being run in front of him, to the horror of his owner if he has won his own course; the ensuing handicap may well be fatal. But the loose dog that has broken away from its handler and joins in a course, coat and lead and all, is another matter; there the fine is richly deserved!

30. NO COURSE

(1) A 'no course' is when by accident or the shortness of the course the dogs are not tried together and if one be then withdrawn the other must run a bye, unless the Judge, on being appealed to, shall decide that it has done enough work to merit exemption.

(2) An 'undecided course' is where the Judge considers the merits of the dogs equal, and if either is then withdrawn, the other cannot be required to run a bye; but the Nominators must at the same time declare which dog remains in.

(3) The Judge shall signify the distinction between a 'no course' by waving his right arm and keeping his hand below the level of the shoulder, and an 'undecided' by taking off his hat.

(4) After an 'undecided' or a 'no course' if the dogs, before being taken up get onto another, or the same, hare the Judge must follow, and must decide in favour of one if he considers that there has been a sufficient trial to justify his doing so.

30. NO COURSE (continued)

(5) A 'no course' or an 'undecided', if claimed on behalf of both dogs, may be run off immediately before the next brace are put into the slips, or in the case of a 'no course' if so ordered by the judge. Otherwise it shall be run again after the next two courses unless it stand over until the next morning when it shall be the first course run; if it is the last course of the day, fifteen minutes shall be allowed after after both dogs have been taken up.

41. OFFENCES

No person shall:

(1) Enter or run a dog other than at an Authorised Coursing Meeting

(2) Run a dog at a Coursing Meeting knowing it is held on land:
  (a) into which hares have been artificially moved during the previous three months or:
  (b) where the hares have not been at liberty during the previous three months or:
  (c) which in the opinion of the Standing Committee is designed to restrict artificially the complete freedom and liberty of hares and such opinion has been published in the Stud Book.

The illustrations show hares being netted on an estate where there was an abundance and where hare shoots were about to take place, for transportation to an area in Yorkshire where there was a shortage. Netting hares is a skilled operation, most difficult being the actual handling of hares from being taken out of the net until being placed in special bowes; unless carried in a certain manner hares will struggle and sometimes die of shock. Handled properly by experts, hares keep still and the damage rate is less than 1 per cent.

Unlike rabbits which bolt straight into a hedge, hares which are driven quietly stop just before a hedge and then go through. Longnets for hares are therefore placed some ten yards out in the next field, the catchers hiding in the ditch under the hedge.

CONSTITUTION and BYE-LAWS

(L) Officers

(4) The Standing Committee shall appoint a courser of repute who will be known as the Senior Stipendiary Steward . . .

(5) The Standing Committee shall appoint Coursing Inspectors annually whose duty will be to inspect coursing grounds prior to a meeting taking place. The Coursing Inspector shall be required to submit to the Senior Stipendiary Steward a report, on the standard form, giving his reasons why he considered a meeting should or should not have taken place.

In simpler language, the Coursing Inspector – one for each Club – is on the side of the hare. He is present throughout each meeting to see fair play – and more than fair play – for the hare and is empowered to stop a beat or even a meeting if he thinks fit. He is responsible for seeing that running grounds are not enclosed to the extent that a hare cannot escape through the hedges or fences; for instance, that if netting is present, either the mesh is large enough for hares to go through or that there is a gap underneath to allow hares to go under but not dogs. He watches to see if hares are coming off a beat with feet balled-up with mud, in which case the the beat must be changed. He is responsible for seeing that the meeting is carried on so as to give the hare the best possible chance of escape.

Chapter 6

PUBLIC COURSING

Having looked at the Rules for organised coursing, which were written for and still govern coursing with greyhounds, let us look briefly at greyhounds and the other three pure breeds that run by these rules, altered in minor ways to suit the characteristics of the dogs concerned.

GREYHOUNDS

The modern greyhound is a sprinter rather than a stayer but coursing writers of the last century spoke of four mile courses as if they were nothing out of the ordinary. Coursing grounds were far more open than they are now, with fewer hedges and walls, and dogs were trained for long courses. In the days before cars, which are lethal to any dog on a public road without a collar and lead and lethal to some which are being safely led, even on minor side roads – how many drivers slow down for you when you are exercising several large lurchers on a side road let alone on a main road? – greyhounds were often exercised in packs, like foxhounds, the trainer being mounted and sometimes with kennel lads on horses; 'slinging along for twenty miles' as one writer describes daily exercise. It is interesting to follow training ideas from the middle of the last century. 'Stonehenge' (Dr J.H.Walsh) writing in 1853, recommended fifteen miles after a horse, increasing to twenty five miles at a trot with at least three to four hours walking about and playing on alternate days. Hugh Dalziel (1886) recommended fifteen to twenty miles and Harding Cox (1892) brought down the mileage to twelve miles on the roads. All three writers recommended hand-slipping for uphill gallops of at least half a mile. Dogs were expected to run up to three or even four courses in a day and the belief was that greyhounds should be as fit as the hares they pursued; 'with my method of training the dog is fit to run as long and as far as any ordinary hare will take him before he is tired, as he must be in order to assess his merits, either in private or in public or both' ('Stonehenge').

Although driven meetings were sometimes held, mainly for the major contests such as the Waterloo Cup, many meetings were walked. The Slipper, most of the trainers and the dog handlers walked as did the 'artisans', with the 'gentry', the landowners, dog owners and probably many of the farmers being mounted. Hence Rule No. 29, which was still in the 1972 copy of the Rule Book:

29. RIDING OVER A DOG

If any person connected with a dog (whether as owner, part-owner, nominator, part-nominator, joint-nominator or trainer or as the servant of any of them) shall, during a course, ride over the opposing dog, the Nominator of the dog so ridden over shall (although the Course be given against it) be deemed the Winner, but shall have the option of allowing the other dog to remain and run out the stake, in which case he shall be entitled to half its winnings.

(By the 1980 edition this Rule had been dropped from the book and replaced by Rule 29, 'Irish Registered Dogs'.)

Coming nearer our own times, Adair Dighton, writing in 1921, recommends not more than six miles road walking, the six miles being done in two hours at first, working up to an hour and a quarter and for the last two weeks before a stake the distance being increased to eight miles.

How long are courses nowadays? Taking two pages at random from the current volume of the Coursing Calendar, of fourteen courses at an East of England meeting the average course was 54.7 seconds and of twenty courses at a Newmarket meeting the average course was 42.7 seconds. These times are taken from the slip to when the course had finished. The dogs do not necessarily stop chasing the hare at that moment but even if one, or both dogs, have got through or over the hedge or wall by which the hare has escaped they will have lost their action and will only be lobbing after the hare with no hope of turning it again, let alone catching it. But in the 42.7 seconds average course from Newmarket, how far has the greyhound galloped? Assuming that he is travelling at a steady 30mph he will cover a mile in two minutes so in 42 seconds he will have galloped less than half a mile, but of course, because of turns, he will not be doing a steady 30mph; how does this compare to his ancestor's three and four mile courses?

With the exception of Colchester, Eley and Epping, most present day greyhound coursing meetings are driven, the only walking being that necessary for clearing the running ground before the beat starts. At a walked meeting the hares inevitably get up in front of the Slipper at very varying distances which make slipping at equal distances difficult. At a driven meeting hares come through from the beat behind the Slipper; he can therefore decide on his slipping distance of between 80 and 120 yards and maintain that distance for every pair of dogs that come to slips during that beat. The problem with driven meetings is the cost. Less than 25 beaters are a waste of time. The most important beaters are those acting as flankers to keep hares going straight forward through the hedge behind which the Slipper is waiting. Anyone can walk down a field waving a flag to get hares on the move but it takes experienced men to keep hares straight and stop them running out. If only five flankers are placed on either side of the beat it leaves fifteen beaters out of the 25 to cover a beat which may extend to 100 acres and often much more. For a successful meeting where hares are fairly plentiful fifty beaters may not be too many. At current rates – 1989 – fifty beaters at £12 to £15 each means a bill of up to £750 to which must be added at least one keeper plus the Judge and Slipper and the hire and transport of the Judge's horse. Entry fees have to be substantial.

A courser of the middle of the last century would notice differences to his sport if he were to attend a present day meeting; the enclosed countryside, the line of cars down the side of the field, only the judge on a horse and communications maintained by portable radios would be some of them. But when he came to look at the dogs he would see a great difference in size between the greyhounds of his day and many modern dogs. Master McGrath, who won the Waterloo Cup in 1868, 1869 and 1871 had a running weight of 54lbs; Coomassie who won the Cup in 1877 and 1878 ran at 44lbs. The running weight of React Fraggl, the 1989 Waterloo Cup winner, was 92lbs, over double the weight of Coomassie and not far short of double Master McGrath's weight. This great increase in size is partly due to park, or enclosed coursing which was run at a few places in England, such as Plumpton, Gosforth, Kempton and Haydock and Wye, racecourses which were easy to enclose. A straight 'running ground' of some 5 furlongs was enclosed with wire netting and large paddocks were formed at either end into which hares were introduced. At meetings, hares were released from the 'holding paddock' one at a time and, having been chased down the course by terriers once or twice a week they knew their way to the escapes into the paddock at the far end. As the ground was enclosed there was little or no room for manoeuvring and most courses only consisted of the run-up and, if the dogs reached the hare in time, the first turn. Park coursing was strictly a betting medium (as it still is in Ireland) and many old-fashioned coursers viewed it with great distrust; it only had a brief existence in England and most of the directors of the various courses were badly hit financially but during its time it undoubtedly did a great deal of harm as dogs were bred for speed alone, not for stamina or working abilities. As a contemporary writer said, 'All must see the ruin that has arisen from it; good greyhounds spoiled, fluky, flashy ones benefited, stamina and determination lost sight of.'

Eventually enclosed coursing became illegal in England, since the hares were confined, but it still holds sway in Ireland where enormous sums of money are wagered. Since speed is everything the bigger dog will usually beat the smaller and as for various reasons, one of which being a doubt about the future of coursing amongst many breeders and trainers, English greyhound bloodlines were allowed to deteriorate in the 1970s, Irish bloodlines, with dogs bred for speed, are producing winners and are therefore fashionable.

WHIPPETS

Whilst the first Club for organised coursing with greyhounds was the Swaffham Club, started in 1776 and still holding some seven meetings a season, organised coursing with whippets did not start until 1962. And whilst show greyhounds and coursing greyhounds are almost two different breeds, having gone their own ways since about 1904 – show greyhounds being registered with the Kennel Club and coursing greyhounds with the Stud Book – show whippets and coursing whippets are the same breed. They are all registered with the Kennel Club, for whatever good that does some of them, and they are dual purpose, many of the whippets which appear regularly on the coursing field also appearing at shows and many of them are winners in both spheres. However, the four clubs for coursing with whippets are not connected in any way with any of the eight whippet breed clubs other than the fact that some of those who course will be members of both coursing and showing clubs.

Whilst the 70lb to 90lb greyhound is an easy match for the 8lb hare if slipped close to – hence the 80 to 100 yard slip to take the edge off the greyhound's speed – the 24lb whippet has to be slipped closer to the hare if there is to be any test of coursing ability. Though not as fast as the greyhound over a distance the whippet has great stamina and will not only run for longer than the average greyhound but will get its tongue in quicker and be ready to run again sooner. The whippet, being smaller and lighter, will turn with the hare and if slipped at not too far from the laid down distance of 'not less than 35 yards' will give a wonderful display of coursing. But if slipped from too far away few whippets have the speed over a distance to come up to a hare and the result is too often a procession, the hare making its way to cover and the whippets following in its wake.

Whippets running under National Whippet Coursing Club Rules have to be 20 inches or under at the shoulder and this rule is strictly adhered to. Whippets have always been 'little dogs' and if allowed to increase in size they lose the whippet type. This can be seen in American whippets and also in some show whippets in England which may measure 22 or 23 inches. The breed standard gives 17½ to 18½ inches for bitches and 18½ to 19½ for dogs as being the ideal height but most show champions of today are nearer two inches higher. There can be a greater relative difference between small and large whippets than in greyhounds and in slips a big whippet can unbalance a small one and even mask its view of the hare. For this reason many stakes for whippets are framed for dogs between certain height or weight brackets. Nevertheless, the good small whippet is perfectly capable of beating dogs two and more inches bigger.

There is no prize money for whippet coursing and in order to keep down costs only one of the four Clubs holds any driven meetings and that towards the end of the season when hares are restless and walked meetings are often unsuccessful. So those who course their whippets have few of the comforts of greyhound coursing, the dog vans close by, the line of cars from which to watch the coursing, the caterer with his tent or mobile kitchen and, above all, the financial ability to hire beaters. There are, however, some advantages; whippets need smaller running grounds than greyhounds and they can run on ground that greyhound owners would avoid, the lighter dogs damaging themselves far less.

Coursing with whippets is an amateur sport. There are no public trainers and there is no money to be won. Because almost all meetings are walked the slipping is inevitably uneven and the greater relative difference in size between whippets means that the bigger dog will often, but by no means always, beat the smaller. But those who do course with whippets very much enjoy their sport.

SALUKIS

The saluki is almost certainly the oldest breed of dog in the world and it remained a pure breed for thousands of years because it was isolated in the deserts of the Middle East. It was accepted by the nomads and treated as part of the family; it was not an outcast as all other dogs are in those parts.

For all its size – and the height is very variable, from 22 to 28 inches – the saluki is not a heavy, muscular dog like the greyhound. Throughout its long history it has had to live on sparse rations and has been used to catch game in dry open country where there are no woods or hedges. The nomads lived in camel-hair tents and for months on end existed on camel milk, dried dates and a little unleavened bread. Only very occasionally, for a guest perhaps, would a camel calf or a goat be killed; herd animals were too valuable to be used for every day eating. So anything that their hunting dogs, salukis, could catch was welcome to men who lived on such a sparse diet. Like its masters, the saluki existed on what it could catch and eat on the spot or what it was given after the men had fed. Desert hares may be put up out of grass tussocks or patches of thorn but gazelle are difficult to get near enough to 'slip' a dog without stalking; not easy to do in open country as anyone will know who has, for instance, tried to course Blackbuck on the Punjab plains. The saluki after a gazelle may well have a very long 'run-up' and it has not therefore needed the speed and power of the greyhound; it is a marathon runner that settles down after its prey, somewhat in the manner of wild dogs in India or Africa, and without the obvious urgency of the greyhound or the whippet.

Although a relative newcomer to England the first Saluki Coursing Club started in the 1920s and, apart from War years, they have been running many meetings each season since then. Saluki coursing is not, perhaps, as spectacular as that with greyhounds or whippets; salukis seldom appear to be running at top speed, probably because they rely on running down whatever they are chasing. Courses are longer and there is less apparent 'work' done by either dog nor does there appear to be the same rivalry; there can even be a degree of co-operation between two dogs as there is between two lurchers who are used to working together. For this reason, judging saluki coursing is more difficult than judging greyhounds or whippets; salukis do not make 'points' so often or so obviously.

Nevertheless, salukis are spectacular dogs to watch at work and there is a very pleasant relaxed atmosphere about Saluki Coursing Club meetings that is sometimes absent from the professional world of the greyhound. Most meetings are walked but one or two driven meetings do take place towards the end of the season. Unlike the whippet coursing clubs, the Saluki Coursing Club is part of the Saluki or Gazelle Hound Club itself.

My personal objection to the saluki is, inevitable from its desert breeding, its independence, for want of a better word. Salukis are not naturally friendly dogs as are greyhounds, whippets and lurchers. There is no obvious desire to please humans which results in the saluki very much pleasing itself as to whether it does what it is told or not. The saluki which comes straight back at the end of a course is in the minority. I know that many greyhounds are difficult to catch at the end of a course but this is because so few of them see a hare except on the occasions on which they run in public; they are excited and want to course another hare. The greyhound that grows up with a lurcher will not only come straight back when called but will often retrieve its hare without much training. Most whippets come back without any trouble and many will retrieve without being taught. The pair of salukis standing over a dead hare in the middle of a ploughed field half a mile away from their owners and taking no notice whatsoever of whistles and calls are by no means rare. But where would the English saluki be now if some saluki owners did not course their dogs? Ruined in one way or another like so many other Kennel Club registered breeds that are no longer given their natural work to do.

DEERHOUNDS

The fourth pure-bred dog used for organised coursing is the Scottish Deerhound. Unlike the saluki who is imported, though it is probably of purer blood and certainly of longer pure-blood than even the greyhound, whippet or deerhound, the latter is a native breed. It evolved to fill a need for a large running dog for deer and, no doubt, wolves and wild boar where they were numerous enough to hunt. To hunt red deer 'cold', unwounded, by sight, over rough, mountainous country in a cold climate a large, rough-coated, strong-footed longdog was needed and that is what the deerhound still is though some that one sees nowadays look as if they would have difficulty walking round the garden.

In the distant past as bows and arrows became more powerful and accurate so coursing deer for food gave way to shooting first and using dogs for following up. Coursing is, after all, a less efficient way of obtaining food than shooting be the quarry deer or hare. Even with a dog after a hare one does not know where the course will finish and whether the hare will be killed and this in the enclosed English countryside. How much more problematic is the dog after a deer, be it red, fallow or roe and be the country farmland and woods or the open hill. At least the deerhound bayed the deer if he – or they, for two were more effective than one – brought it 'to bay' and the hunter had a good chance of coming up with them. Dogs that attacked red deer other than on the move did not usually last long as red deer can inflict fatal wounds both with antlers and front feet. I understand that some HPR gundogs will bay a wounded deer or a freshly dead one but though they may well exist I have never heard of a lurcher that would bay a deer which it had cornered. One can say that deer 'coursed' by lurchers are usually smaller than the red deer and more easily brought down – though not necessarily killed – but although it is not technically illegal the man who runs deer with dogs will sooner or later end up in court and what easier way to be found out in the over-populated English countryside than one, or two dogs baying a deer?

But back to the deerhound. Bows and arrows and spears gave way to matchlocks and flintlocks and still the deerhound, or at any rate a dog to do the same work was needed. For various reasons the pure deerhound became scarce when the somewhat more accurate guns with some rifling became popular and collie crosses or even pure collies were used for following up wounded deer. Then came the accurate high velocity rifle and the need for a dog had disappeared; dogs were no longer taken on the hill. Apart from the more fatal wound delivered by the rifle, a dog meant that another man had to follow up necessarily closer than the pony man and if a dog was slipped then no one knew where he and the deer would finish up and how many more deer they would disturb. So the deerhound's work was ended, apart from those bred by a few landowners who still coursed deer in the more out of the way parts of Scotland.

The resurrection of the Scottish deerhound was slow but it was surely done by devoted breeders, even though the 1936–45 War left too few strains in the U.K. for breeding. Old-new blood was brought back from America and an outcross was made to coursing greyhounds. Finally, and just as important, a coursing branch of the Breed Club was started in the 1950s to retain the hunting instinct and retain true soundness in deerhounds. The Deerhound Coursing Club runs under slightly altered N.C.C. Rules and courses the Brown hare in England and the Blue Hare in Scotland, often over ground so rough that some lurcher owners might hesitate to run their dogs.

The deerhound is the largest of the longdogs, the bitches being from 27 to 28 inches and the dogs from 30 inches to about 33 inches. In coursing they somewhat resemble salukis in that there is not the same sense of urgency that one sees with greyhounds and whippets. They are slower out of slips, they sometimes hardly seem to be pulling at their collars at all and partly because of their very large and apparently slower stride they do not seem to be galloping flat out. But from the meetings I have been to most of the dogs – or rather *hounds* as they are more properly called – seem to be enjoying themselves and certainly their owners do. Their size handicaps them where hares are concerned but that is not their fault.

Chapter 7

PRIVATE COURSING

There may be a few people who still course 'privately' with greyhounds; a certain amount of private coursing is done with whippets by those who have the land or access to land where such things are possible but it really amounts to no more than going for a walk with the dogs and if a hare gets up the dogs chase it. Most people who want to course with pure-bred longdogs join an existing club to do so; this is because land where hares can be coursed becomes harder to find year by year. So when one talks about private coursing one really means coursing with lurchers; but unlike pure bred longdogs, cross-bred longdogs, lurcher-longdogs were never meant to 'course', to give the hare 'law' and to score points. They were bred to hunt, jump, catch, kill and carry, to find and catch a hare as quickly and as economically as possible, bring it back and be ready for another run.

The difference between the lurcher and the 'pure' longdog goes back eight centuries, back to the imposition of Norman game laws on the native Saxons. Under Norman law, all land belonged to the King and with the land went everything on it, the game and the timber, the *venison* and the *vert*. To preserve the game, strict laws governed the keeping of dogs that were capable of killing deer. They were rough times, life was cheap and it was recognised that guard dogs were needed against robbers and malefactors but those living in, or within a certain distance of, a forest were only allowed to keep dogs above a certain size, i.e., dogs that could guard house and property, if their feet were 'lawed' by having one or more front toes chopped off so that they could not chase deer.

Dogs that could kill deer by running them down, the smooth or rough greyhounds of the time, could only be kept by persons of certain rank; lords and barons and, interestingly enough, bishops and abbots. If the common man, be he freeman or serf, was found with a greyhound he was liable to punishments which varied from fines to being flayed alive. The common man of the time was still Saxon by blood and Saxon in outlook; the dilution of Saxon blood by Norman blood came gradually. He saw no reason why he should be prevented from killing deer to provide meat for himself and his family and he continued to hunt the King's deer despite the threat of the death penalty. But to save himself from being caught in the first and most obvious trap he diluted the blood of his greyhound, and therefore its looks, by crossing it with the village dog or cattle dog, in other words he bred and used what we now call a lurcher. He had a dog that was capable of catching deer, particularly if the deer was first wounded by a spear or an arrow, and if the dog grew up to look too much like a greyhound then he probably chopped off its tail so that at a distance it looked like a sheep dog or cattle dog.

Even down to the reign of Queen Anne the prohibition remained against the keeping of greyhounds by those not qualified by rank or property; the lurcher continued to be the hunting dog of the villager and the poacher and the gypsy, though the lurcher was at work in England at least 200 years before the first gypsies arrived from the Continent. As time went by others, landowners and those who had the ground to hunt and course with them, kept lurchers as well as greyhounds, and sometimes in their place, as sporting dogs. It is probably not an exaggeration to say that this remained the place of the lurcher until the early 1970's when with the start and then flourishing of lurcher shows the cross-bred dog became known to an infinitely wider circle, many of whom were – and are – not countrymen. It was probably inevitable that amongst the new lurcher owners were some who were looking for new forms of petty crime. From robbing gas-meters, breaking into cars and mugging old people it is a short step to trespassing in search of game with lurchers and of course it is very much more fun. It was also inevitable that as law abiding new lurcher owners looked for more and more places where they could run their dogs so the hooligans with lurchers gave the lurcher a worse and worse name by their trespassing and poaching, often accompanied by violence if they were approached.

Poaching has always been a fact of rural life; illegal coursing has always gone on but the spread of motorways has given poaching gangs far greater mobility and it is nothing now for a gang caught poaching in Lincolnshire to be found to have come from as far away as Dover or Bristol. As well as motorways the four-wheel-drive vehicle means that the poacher need no longer walk to look for hares. His FWD car or pick-up takes him off the tarmac and across fields and if the police eventually do appear then he drives straight off again onto the road and no longer has to *run* away. Another reason for illegal coursing today, or at least trespass in search of hares, is the practice of giving a racing greyhound a 'sharpener'. If a dog that has potential speed but for various reasons is not winning races is given a run after a live hare and gets his teeth into some 'fur' it may well be that the next time out on the track he will run with much greater zeal, resulting in a betting *coup*. One hears nowadays from farmers and 'keepers in hare country of offers varying from a bottle of whisky to £100 and more in cash for the opportunity to run a track greyhound at a hare. It is not the established trainers who do this but there are such things as unlicensed tracks. The trouble is that to a farmer or a 'keeper, some men with longdogs walking across the fields looking for hares are always taken to be lurcher people and so the lurcher gets the blame for poaching done with greyhounds.

It so happened that the extraordinary rise in the number of lurchers and their new owners' understandable wish to run their dogs somewhere, anywhere, coincided with a continuing decline in the hare population. As I have already said, this has mainly been caused by modern farming practices and the agri-business of growing vast prairies of corn with its ever increasing use of chemicals. Fewer hares mean fewer farms where coursing can take place; even the old established greyhound coursing clubs are finding that their running grounds diminish in number. It might be thought that small groups of people with a few lurchers do not need the space that an organised meeting under rules needs but they are up against the fact that a walked meeting needs more ground than a driven meeting. Some lurcher clubs have tried renting ground for a day's coursing but suitable ground is very difficult to find, hares can and do move according to how the weather changes and it is very doubtful if any farmer would make set-aside money from renting out land for coursing though I know of one landowner who is doing just this for the greyhound club of which he is Chairman.

But to happier matters, legal coursing with lurchers, or cross bred longdogs.

In public coursing the object is to test one dog against another, by slipping them at a set distance after a hare whose actions are unpredictable. It may run straight and fast, it may twist and turn, courses may be long or short and luck may play its part. The winner of a stake will run from three courses in an 8-dog stake to six courses in a 64-dog stake, spread over three days, and it is usually the best dog which wins. But what is the object of private coursing?

The object will vary with the people concerned. It can be dog versus dog, as in public coursing or dog versus hare, almost always as a betting medium – 'best of three hares'. It can be to kill hares, particularly where the landowner or farmer does not have time for or does not want a hare shoot. This is the most humane method of hare control as the hares are either killed quickly or get away unwounded and the weaklings are weeded out; something that no hare shoot can do. Or it may be just for the pleasure of seeing one's dogs doing what they are bred for: working after hares. As with the objects, the methods will vary. At the 'top' there is the the organised meeting complete with slipper and judge; at the 'bottom' there are the poaching gangs (though some will not agree with the placing!). In the middle comes the half-mile long line of owners each slipping their own dogs as hares get up; but first the organised meeting.

At its most formal this will be a group of lurcher owners – sometimes called a club – who will arrange meetings through the season on various farms, often giving dates well ahead. A licensed slipper may be employed or one of the members will slip the dogs in pairs; the dogs wear red and white collars as in proper coursing and they will usually be led in single slips as some lurchers will not walk quietly if held too close to a strange dog in double slips. There is a judge who will give his decision by waving a red or white handkerchief in the usual manner. As the judge is on foot, not mounted, he can only judge from one position on the field and his decisions may not always be strictly accurate but no matter. I once asked the late Jack Chadwick what he would do about judging lurchers; he said, 'How many points for a good retrieve?'

Next comes an equally controlled lurcher meeting but without slipper or judge. The two dogs to run are led by their owners some 20 yards ahead of the walking line and they agree on which should give the word to slip when a hare gets up. At both these meetings someone is in charge, the hare is given law, only two dogs are slipped at a time, the line is kept straight and everyone stands still while a course is being run until the two dogs are taken up and the next pair are ready in slips. When I say that control is strict, I know of at least two such groups of lurcher owners where any unsporting behaviour or mis-behaviour results in that person being banned from any further meetings.

A third type of 'organised' coursing with lurchers is often held where the country is more open and the hedges are few and far between. The purpose may be just the pleasure of seeing dogs running or it may be to kill hares for the farmer or landowner who has not the time or the desire to have a hare shoot. The 'line' may be anything up to half a mile long, which makes control difficult, owners slip their own dog or dogs as hares get up, hoping that the hare will be retrieved and that their dogs will not see another course going on and join in. Given *some* form of organisation and discipline this can be a very efficient method of hare control and I have seen over fifty hares killed on the broad acres of Bedfordshire before the lunch break. But it does mean that without some control the line may or may not stand still while a course is taking place and there is no certainty that only two dogs will be slipped; distance between dog owners makes this almost impossible. A hare gets up at the left of the line and two dogs go. Whilst they are coursing – perhaps out of sight of many present – a hare gets up on the right and two dogs are slipped. Then a hare gets up in the centre of the line and someone lets his two dogs go without thinking so there are six dogs on the move. The most dogs I have seen running at one time was nine, not all after one hare, but the danger of this sort of 'coursing' is over-running dogs. Lurchers can run a long way over open country before killing or losing their hare, and on the way back may well see another course being run; unless a dog is absolutely exhausted it will usually join in until *that* course finishes and may even join in on a third course before it can be picked up. This can be a very efficient method of hare control but it can be hard on dogs and I have seen many lurchers grossly over-run. One of the problems in lurcher coursing is that few lurcher owners have the time and facilities of the greyhound trainer and lurchers are seldom as fit as they ought to be for coursing. The old idea that a dog should be as fit as the hare it courses applies to very few modern lurchers.

Another of my dislikes is slipping dogs when the hare is near a hedge or other cover or perhaps about to disappear over a hill. I like to see my dogs working and I have never seen the point of slipping where the ensuing course will not be seen.

Finally comes what is now called 'match coursing', dog versus hare, 'best of three hares', etc, on which large sums of money are laid. This, of course, goes against the spirit of coursing because the object is to kill hares as a betting medium, not to 'estimate the value of the work done by each dog'. Challenges are issued and there is currently much debate about the best crosses for matches. There is agreement that greyhound must be a major part of the cross and the argument is between deerhound and saluki for

79

the other half or whatever proportion is being argued about. But whatever the best breeding may be there is another side to this problem, for problem it is.

Those who advocate, promote and write about 'matches' and 'match dogs' are, in fact, advocating and promoting poaching and, because of the sums of money involved, poaching with violence. They may think that their publicised breeding programmes for match dogs will only lead to matches being run where permission has been obtained (though I find it difficult to believe each apparent innocence); but any debate on the subject merely encourages the increasing number of urban louts who look on any open ground that might hold hares as theirs for the entering. I suspect that the match promoters are against private ownership of land; they have only to talk to 'keepers to find out what they are encouraging and when I use the word 'louts' I do not mean the usual picture of the football hooligan. The 'match lout' can just as easily arrive in a Mercedes, BMW or even Ferrari, accompanied by hangers-on in vans, 4WD cars and pick-ups with the dogs. Those handling the money may well not be English and their followers are often thugs. A suitable field is seen, one or two men walk a dog and if a hare gets up the dog is slipped. If the 'keeper appears and manages to capture the dog he is told that if he does not let the dog go his own kennels will be 'sorted out'. Faced by such odds he has no option.

Still, the countryside is changing rapidly, developers move in where no one would have imagined houses being built, roads and motorways are spreading, more and more townspeople are demanding a place in the country to live and then demanding that the countryside conforms to their idea of what it should be. Their views on wild animals are based on sentimental misunderstanding and their attitudes to country sports range from indifference to abhorrence. It may not be long before coursing as we have known it is only a memory.

THE BOBBERY PACK

I was born and brought up to hunting and learned stable work the hard way from an early age but my interest was divided equally between watching hounds work and riding across country. I had also been interested in coursing from about the age of fifteen and had owned greyhounds in partnership with our village butcher, so my coursing interest goes back almost as long as hunting. But much as I have always enjoyed and still enjoy public and private coursing, either running a dog of my own or watching good dogs run, whatever longdogs they are, I am quite sure sure that my best days have been when out with my own bobbery pack.

'Bobbery' is an Anglo-Indian slang word meaning a noise or a disturbance, the earliest written examples coming from about 1700; the derivation is probably from the Hindi, *'Bap-re'*, 'Oh Father, look!' and it describes the local reaction to the most unconventional 'Bobbery Packs' which hunted the area around many

Indian Cantonments except for those which had their own conventional packs of hounds: Poona, Peshawar, Ootacamund etc. A Bobbery Pack was a collection of every sort of dog, a scratch pack of greyhounds, kangaroo hounds, terriers, foxhounds, dachshunds, bull-terriers (very popular dogs with British soldiers) and even the odd gundog; any dog that any Soldier or Civilian could bring along to hunt jackal, fox or hare. They hunted on Sunday mornings in the monsoon season when other forms of exercise were difficult or impossible, some 'packs' being hunted on foot and others on horseback, and the proportion of longdogs, yap-dogs and smell-dogs varied with the country over which they hunted. Here, in the increasingly confined and over-populated English countryside, smell-dogs and yap-dogs are not needed as they make too much noise; the last thing one wants. One terrier is quite enough and with a couple of good whippets that will follow rabbit runs through hedges one can probably dispense with a terrier; I have run a bobbery pack made up of longdogs and whippets since leaving the Army in 1962.

To me, the essence of such 'hunting' is that it should be solitary; the whole object is defeated by a crowd. One should be on one's own or at the most with one or two other people, people who will keep quiet because the human voice scares 'game' even up-wind and a female voice can get hares on the move three and four fields away. On one's own one makes no plan other than deciding which direction to start in, one turns left or right at a whim, one carries on or goes home according to what happens. What does happen may be nothing, anything or everything. For some 20 years I have kept a rough diary of coursing meetings, steeplechasing, point to points, hunting, interesting birds, etc, seen and, above all, days out with the dogs. I will quote from some of the entries of these days to show how varied one's 'hunting' can be; the 'pack' consisted of up to four longdogs, three whippets and a terrier when all were present but this was not always the case, various members being lame or in season, off work or left behind for some other reason. Also, since dogs lives are, sadly, much shorter than our own, pack membership inevitably changes over the years as some grow too old to hunt and eventually die and others are born or brought in in their place.

Rabbits have almost disappeared round here and we have hardly seen one, let alone hunted one for about four years. Hares numbers are certainly not what they were ten years ago; where I could count on seeing up to half a dozen hares in certain fields and always some hares on every farm where I had permission to take the dogs, they are now few and even the local pack of beagles may draw for an hour and more before finding. For various reasons, changes in farming practices, farms changing hands, shooting syndicates etc, I have lost two thirds of the land I walked the dogs over 20 years ago but with increasing age and fewer dogs I do not really feel the loss now. Hence the fun of looking back through the hunting diaries and re-reading about triumph and failure, good days and bad, legal and illegal happenings. Entries are necessarily brief and condensed and in quoting I have to fill in some of the gaps. I start with a badger.

Badgers are common in these parts and I know of up to a dozen occupied setts within a few miles; I visit them from time to time to see whether they are still occupied or whether they have been disturbed though I certainly do not do so on behalf of any so-called badger-watch group or other do-gooders. As a matter of interest, many of the local badgers are brown and dark yellow, rather than the traditional black and white. Knowing badgers as I do I would never dream of intentionally letting the dogs go anywhere near one; unlike foxes badgers do little or no harm, they keep themselves to themselves and they have a bite that can cripple a dog.

On a very cold and wet day in March, in the mid-1970s, I took the dogs out for a walk round the edge of a big estate where I had worked for some years; I had, of course, permission then to go over the adjacent farmland. The steady and almost horizontal rain turned from time to time to snow and sleet; only a sense of duty to exercise the dogs made me go out at all. We were walking along the headland of a ploughed field, slightly sheltered by a belt of trees, and the dogs taking what cover they could behind me. Passing a patch of lantana bushes the dogs suddenly threw up their heads and dived into the thicket; there was an instant row and thinking that they had got a fox I shouted to them to hurry up as I wanted to get home. Far from a quick end, the noise increased and on pushing into the middle of the bushes I saw that they were piling over and round a badger which seemed to be held by something. As I arrived the badger broke loose from whatever had been holding it and the melee moved rapidly into the open. They were 50 yards out on the ploughed field before I managed to get collars and leads on the big dogs and it was another three or four minutes before I had got them all, whippets and the terrier included, safely tethered to fence posts; the fact that it was a very run-down farm and sound fence posts were few and far between made things more difficult. Going back to the badger I found it lying still, but full of fight and with no visible damage other than what looked like a snare round its neck; by this time I was as plastered with wet mud as were dogs and badger and the problem arose of moving it back into cover. I had done a fair amount of digging for badgers when I was young – to move them from where they were not wanted to a safer place – and I knew how to 'tail' a badger but not when the animal's tail and my hands were slippery with mud. I managed to move it eventually and saw that there was a locked snare round its neck but I had no means of holding it still, even if I had had a pair of wire-cutters in my pocket, so I left it by the stream and went to look where the dogs had found it. There, in the middle of a trodden circle of earth, was a short length of chain pegged to the ground with a broken piece of snare wire bolted to it; the badger must have been there for several hours if not more from the footmarks. I had a quick look at the dogs, found that the damage could have been worse and then went back to see what I could do for the badger but it had moved into the wood. I knew that the nearest wire-cutters were at least a quarter of an hour away, there was no way of following up the badger with the dogs I had, there seemed to be nothing else that I could usefully do and hindsight has not suggested anything. When I had first seen the badger I wondered what on earth it was doing there at eleven o'clock in the morning; the next question was the snare; who had set it and why there? Had it been for a fox or for a badger? In the circumstances there was no way of finding out.

From one forbidden animal to another though in a different county. I had gone to stay for a night or two with relations, taking *Tarn*, her daughter *Rummage* aged eleven months and *Witchet*, one of the whippets, with me. Walking round the farm the next day I noticed the dogs feathering along the edge of a plot of maize as if on the line of something. Turning into the next field, of bare arable, I started to put them on leads just in case, and had got the whippet into her collar when a pair of roe deer bounced out of the thick hazel hedge some 70 yards ahead. They trotted off with their usual high step and of course *Tarn* and *Rummage* went straight after them. Nearing what I knew was a very thick old cover the roe divided, one going to the left followed by *Tarn* and the other straight on into the thicket with *Rummage* close behind. Thinking I'd better deal with what I could see I watched *Tarn* follow her roe round three sides of the 30 acre field, luckily not going onto a public footpath or adjacent farmland, and she rolled it over in the ditch not 50 yards from me. I got her collar and lead on as quickly as I could, checking that the roe was dead – with no visible marks she had presumably broken its neck – and set off to the wood. I knew the area well and by following a path leading straight in I found *Rummage* with the other roe, also dead; from the venery point of view it was not a bad effort for a puppy. Local circumstances being what they were there was nothing I could do about the roe deer; they were unlikely to be found for a day or two and the many foxes round about would feed well but it was a waste of good meat.

In these parts we do not have roe or fallow deer – I have always been glad of the fact – but Muntjac, or Barking Deer are common enough to be a pest. They were escapees from Woburn, getting out from the Park before the 1914 War and spreading far and wide ever since; they can be and often are found in hedgerows, bramble patches and even gardens, as well as in almost every wood. Our 3 acre garden seems to be on a muntjac 'roadway' from one large wood to another and the dogs have killed many of them in the garden and outside. They make good eating but with their sharp fangs pointing downwards – with which they fight one another – they can damage small dogs and are best left alone if seen first; apart from anything else dogs seldom kill them quickly.

Foxes are a problem here. As our local pack of hounds no longer meets in the village, seldom runs this way and to the best of my knowledge have not killed a fox in the parish for at least five years, those who keep sheep or poultry have to take their own measures to keep the fox population down. Over the years the dogs have found foxes in hedges, in thickets, in patches of brambles, in hollow trees, in the open in daylight and by lamplight at night. Some are chased and killed, others get away but they do not give much sport with longdogs; the big lurcher or greyhound that cannot catch a fox in a short distance is not worth keeping. One episode involving a fox is worth telling as it shows how a dog can work out problems for itself.

For a couple of months one summer I was asked to keep an eye out for strangers on a shooting estate between one 'keeper going and his replacement arriving. At about a quarter to ten on a July evening I had been having a late look-round and was walking quietly back towards the car; I had *Tarn*, then aged seven, with me. We came up to the corner of a spinney and I saw *Tarn*, who was off the lead and just ahead of me, suddenly freeze. Looking round the corner I saw a hare some 30 yards ahead on the edge of the gravel track. *Tarn* had started off after the hare which dodged past her, came back past me and went through the hedge into a field of wheat. I could hear a course going on in the wheat and after half a minute the hare came back through the hedge, along the track and into a smaller field of wheat on the left, with *Tarn* five yards or so behind it. I waited at the corner of the spinney, knowing that she would turn up sooner or later – she knew the area well – and looked around with field glasses, it being nearly dark. Down to my right I saw a fox come out of the spinney some 50 yards away and trot across the fallow towards where *Tarn* and the hare had disappeared into the corn. He reached the track and stood for a minute or two, looking round and sniffing the air, and then sat down and seemed to be listening to something in the wood beyond the strip of wheat. *Tarn* had been away for some time when through the glasses I saw her coming back through the corn on the left with her head high, carrying a hare; the fox obviously heard her but could not make out what the noise was. When she was a few yards from the edge of the corn the fox cub, for that was what it was but well grown, turned and trotted back across the fallow towards the spinney from where it had come. *Tarn* came out onto the track, put down the hare and sniffed at the spot where the fox had sat. Looking up she saw the fox halfway back to the wood and she started off after it at full gallop, disappearing into the wood almost on its heels. I heard some crashing in the undergrowth and *Tarn* reappeared carrying the fox cub which she brought up to me and dropped it at my feet. Then, without a pause she trotted back along the track, picked up the hare and brought that in turn to where I had been standing all this time, laying it beside the cub, all without a word from me. At seven years old and 'pig-fat' from a false pregnancy this was a good effort, but *Tarn* was easily the most intelligent dog I have ever been lucky enough to own – or perhaps she owned me.

While on the subject of foxes, I see from past entries that damage from fox bites was worst when I had neglected to wash wounds as quickly as possible with hot Dettol or other disinfectant. Foxes teeth are extremely sharp, far sharper than dogs' teeth, and carry infection, probably from eating carrion; puncture wounds, particularly on dogs' faces, can blow up very quickly. I only remember one occasion when a bite from a fox put a lurcher on the sidelines for a couple of months and that was a bite through the knee, puncturing the synovial sac. The dog had to go onto 'bute' before it was sound enough to work again.

Entries about hares are far too numerous to quote; 'found in such-and-such a field, so-and-so took the hare up the far side of the hedge to the gate where the others joined in' repeated many times makes dull reading but one remembers the odd occasion when something unexpected occurred. Two of us wanted to give some whippets a gallop as they were due to run at a coursing meeting and because of frosted ground were short of fast work. We slipped *Ruff* and *Honey* on a hare at about 60 yards, thinking that it would take them for a run but they would not catch it. As the two whippets went down a big field towards a farm road 200 yards away we heard hounds to our left and down the gravel road came about half the local pack, presumably after a fox which we had not noticed; they were spread out over about 100 yards. The hare went straight on through a gap behind the leaders, three more hounds passed along the track, over at right-angles through the next gap went the two whippets, the remaining hounds passed on along the track and the whippets disappeared through a hedge. So far as we could see neither hare, hounds nor whippets took the slightest notice of each other, each intent on their own business, hare escaping, hounds following a scent and whippets coursing by sight. No Hunt Staff or field appeared and I never did find out exactly why hounds were running at that particular place and time. On another occasion, on the same estate, two of us were running lurchers and a hare had gone into a spinney. As we started to call the two dogs out we heard hounds on the far side of the small wood and along the wood side came the Whipper-in and two hunting farmers with others, including the Huntsman and one of the Masters appearing up a farm road. A certain amount of discussion ensued, somewhat pointed on both sides, and it turned out that for some reason the Meet and draw had been changed over-night. I later heard that my son-in-law, who did not happen to be hunting that day, was told that his subscription might have to be doubled if his father-in-law insisted on drawing the same coverts with lurchers as hounds were using!

In the well wooded and strongly fenced and hedged countryside where I live one does not always see the whole of a run with one's dogs and sometimes one can only guess what happened. I see that in the middle of one January I wrote that the thermometer had stood steady at around 30 degrees since the beginning of the month and that on the 16th the temperature was 22 degrees with about four inches of snow. We went down the long meadow below the house with several of the dogs 'pointing' at the left hand hedge. Over the fence and stream at the bottom and off the dogs went right handed along the stream; the two lurchers going straight on across the next meadow and the two whippets turning left handed up the hedge to the top and back again. I could not see any hare, fox or muntjac footmarks in the snow but the dogs may well have covered what there was. With the whippets I followed the lurchers over the next field to the lane where one of the lurchers, *Hettie*, came out of Dunkley's big field, panting hard, and led us back again obviously on a line of something. *Tarn* and *Hettie*, and the two whippets, *Treacle* and *Willow*, cast around in the snow and a hare got up from mid-field and made for the thick hedge into the old allotments. I went back onto the lane with the terrier and was joined by *Treacle* who came out of the allotments; five minutes later *Willow* arrived from behind me and then *Rummage* appeared trotting along the lane from the direction of Dunkley's farm, panting hard and with a long cut down her muzzle. No sign of *Hettie* and although *Willow* wanted to take a line across the field opposite the allotments I put them all on leads as they had had enough for the morning; *Tarn*, aged 13, had got cramp in a hind leg. Halfway back towards the house *Hettie* joined us, blowing hard. Where had she been and, indeed, where had *Rummage* been and what were they all chasing?

Another 'unseen' occurred one February when I had taken four lurchers and two whippets up to — Barn for a quiet walk. Starting off down the track to the valley the two whippets slipped through the hedge on my left before I could stop them – many whippets are experts at this form of evasion – and when I got to the bend in the track the lurchers went away left handed; I assumed that they had heard the whippets giving tongue. I turned left handed after them and met *Tarn* coming back; I could see the other three lurchers working down the far hedge. Crossing the stream at the bottom by the sleeper bridge and starting across Rape Field *Hettie* joined us and was put on a lead with *Tarn*. Approaching the bottom of Quill Copse we were joined by *Rummage*, very tired and with blood on her face and whiskers. She had obviously caught and killed something after a long course. We carried on round the bottom of Quill Copse where one of the whippets, *Witchet* arrived from behind us so I turned back. Halfway across Rape Field to the sleeper bridge the other whippet, *Minnie*, came from the direction of Hill Spinney and as we reached the bridge the fourth lurcher, *Gypsy*, arrived from behind us, her face also covered in blood like *Rummage*; she, too, was temporarily exhausted and sicked up some mucus and thin guts. That evening the 'keeper phoned to thank me for dealing with a fox with which he had been having trouble. It turned out that he had seen *Gypsy* and *Rummage* killing a fox near the pheasant release pen that afternoon so that answered the question of what they had chased and where they had been but it was curious that none of them had smelt of fox when they got back to me as is usually the case. I remember one of the whippets, little black *Treacle*, helping to kill a fox by seizing and shaking a back leg, only to receive a shower of urine all over her.

Of course not every day's 'hunting' was unseen. Amongst many others, one January at Botolph Claydon, in very heavy going on wet arable, Sue Sowerby's *Willow* and my *Hettie* were slipped on a hare at Middle Farm. It was a long slip and, as a result, a fairly straight course with only about four turns. They went in full view, over a sheep wire fence, over a barbed wire fence, through a boundary hedge, over the Hogshaw Lane, over another barbed wire fence, past Fulbrook Farm and up Quainton Hill where they presumably lost the hare amongst gorse bushes at the top. One of the party with field glasses gave us a running commentary from which we knew that the dogs were never more than a few yards behind the hare even though they had to jump several wire fences and gallop up a steepening hill; from the map it was a good mile run to where they disappeared over the brow of the hill and on the way back they still had to jump the same fences though this time down hill.

Hettie may have looked like a walking hearth rug but although she was not as fast as *Gypsy* or her litter sister *Rummage* she had almost unlimited stamina and many of her hares were run down, rather than caught 'on the run-up'. At one lurcher day in East Anglia we were slipping one dog at a time. When *Hettie's* turn came she set off after her hare and after several turns disappeared round the corner of a wood. One of the party who was following in a Land Rover because of a recent hip operation went off after her and eventually came back to say that he had found her a mile and a half away, lying with both front feet on the hare and waiting till she had got enough breath back to deal with it.

This was a hare-killing day for the landowners and I see that the total was 34. Considering how flat and open the land was, with no hedges at all, and that dogs were being run singly, on their own, on fit, February hares, this was a lot of hares killed by about 16 longdogs. There was no question of betting on the 'best of so many'; we had been asked to thin out hares for various landowners in the area and I see from the diary that the total for four days between the 20th January and the 6th February, mostly with the same dogs, was 144 hares. They had been coursed and killed quickly, the weaklings had been weeded out and the fit hares had escaped to breed that Spring, a result that no hare shoot could produce.

I have already suggested that the spread of so-called civilization into the countryside may stop coursing except on certain big estates, possibly in my life time. It has already happened in these parts where a bobbery pack in concerned. More and more non-country people have moved into the area, more and more of them think that they can exercise their dogs anywhere they please and they are horrified at the thought of anything in the nature of country sports. Longdog men who live in wild places should make the most of their sport while it lasts.

In the Winter of 1978–79 there was some correspondence in certain 'country magazines' on the subject of poaching, of course including poaching with lurchers. Despite the fact that poaching has continued for 800 years and has not yet been stopped, people thought that something ought to be seen to be done and as part of the 'action' I joined Sandy Mackenzie, of the Coursing Supporters Club, and Peter Baillie, of the British Deer Society, in London for a 'working lunch' to discuss the problem. On the way home in the train I wrote a Coursing Code which was tidied up and approved by the National Coursing Club, the three other pure-breed Coursing Clubs, the British Field Sports Society and, eventually I believe, by the British Deer Society. I doubt if anyone has looked at the Coursing Code since then and I will not quote the whole of it but it did say that, 'Those who course with a recognised club will be coursing under rules which have stood the test of time and which are up-dated and revised as circumstances require' and, 'Everybody coursing privately will be guided by their conscience, but we urge that at all times they show the sense of responsibility expected in a country sportsman'. In the Code of Conduct which follows, No. 4 states, 'Never loose more than two dogs on a hare and always give sufficient law'.

I quote this because it has been my experience that two longdogs are the optimum number for coursing a hare and that the more than two there are the more they get in each others' way. I can still picture an occasion when two of us, with three lurchers and seven whippets all loose, were walking across a stubble field which was dotted with straw bales, yet to be carted. A hare got up in mid-field and made for a wood at the far end. A whippet was the first to spot it and the rest joined in. Dodging round straw bales and sometimes running straight through the pack the hare reached the wood and safety without being touched so far as we could see; after each scrimmage half the dogs were looking round to see which way the hare had gone. I remember other occasions when three or more dogs have failed to catch a hare through muddling each other.

On an estate in Hertfordshire where I have been privileged to course for some 25 years, hares on a certain field almost always run up the slope and right handed into a strip of woodland at the top. In Plate 244 I show a hare coursed by two lurchers which appeared to slow down and turn away from the wood every time the dogs got near; it then spun round on its hind legs and was away towards the wood. The hare repeated this identical manoeuvre four times and got to the wood with yards to spare over the lurchers. I suspected that it had used this trick before but I think it was the first time I had seen a hare turning round from dogs upright on its hind legs. One does of course see this when hares are sparring in Spring.

Unless one sticks grimly to road work, exercising longdogs out of the official coursing season inevitably means that some hares are found and coursed and a few killed but we did not deliberately go out looking for them between the middle of March and the middle of September. Certainly I lost one lurcher, *Hettie*, from heat-stroke, when they all got off after a hare that was in a most unexpected place on the first really hot day in July. *Hettie* had an extremely shaggy coat and was due for her annual clip either that day or the next. A very long gallop along farm tracks with corn growing high on either side and not a breath of wind was too much for her and when I eventually reached them *Hettie* was swaying on her feet. The farmer through whose yard they had gone very kindly picked her up with a tractor but it was too late even to put her into a cattle trough. Which brings me to the subject of *obedience* in longdogs and here I do differentiate between longdogs and lurchers. Depending on their work, some lurchers do need to be highly trained for what they are to do whereas most longdogs can do with less training unless they are to be used for demonstrations, etc.

I freely admit that I am not a dog trainer, other than insisting on basic obedience, a dog knowing its name, going to its bed when told to do so, walking calmly on a lead and being safe with all farm stock, including our own bantams. Coming when called is obviously necessary under normal conditions but none of my dogs would stop coursing a hare – or fox, etc – if I called and, to be honest, I would not expect them to do so. On the day that *Hettie* died, her sister *Rummage* had gone off with her followed by a whippet and the only one to stop when I shouted and whistled was old *Tarn* who had more sense than to try and catch a hare in that temperature.

Obviously a longdog/lurcher must retrieve what it catches but I have never tought retrieving a dummy beyond the first stages. All my dogs – including the whippets at times – have retrieved rabbits and hares so long as they were coursing on their own or with a strange dog. Some retrieves have been done from very long distances. On one occasion I measured on a map a retrieve made by *Gypsy* and it came out at almost a mile in a straight line; she had been running against a strange dog which had dropped out half way. This was by no means her only long retrieve and her doing this was the more unusual in that she was the complete longdog. She looked like a black greyhound, her father had been a semi-finalist in the Waterloo Cup, her grandfather and great grandfather had both won the Cup and her maternal great grandfather had held many records at Newcastle and other Northern tracks; not the breeding from which one would expect long retrieves but the brains came from her mother, *Tarn*, and the long tail-female line of lurchers. One of *Gypsy*'s litter brothers, *Paddy*, who also looked like a black greyhound and stood some 27 inches at the shoulder, became an outstanding lamping dog despite his coursing greyhound father. In the same way both *Tarn*'s other daughters who I kept, *Hettie* and *Rummage* were by a lurcher, Mick White's *Lucky*, and they retrieved as a matter of course if they were running on their own or against a strange dog but if the whole pack caught anything edible I had to run fast if I wanted any share of it. Hares and rabbits would be divided quickly and eaten on the spot.

I think that my doubts about obedience training for lurchers stems from watching the obedience tests that feature at Crufts and other dog shows and which are shown on television; the dog, usually a collie of sorts, walking along with its head curled round its handler's left knee and with its face up, watching his hand held in front of his chest – actually I suppose that I should say 'her hand' and 'her chest' as most obedience people seem to be women. To me a dog should be watching its front and if it is not on a lead it should be able to jump straight into a gallop if a hare gets up. If this is not what is needed then the dog should be on a lead or a slip lead. I have great admiration for people such as Tony Diprose and Dennis Eastwood who give obedience demonstrations with lurchers but I have not got the patience or knowledge to do it myself nor, secretly, do I really want to. If I have a somewhat romantic image of the longdog 'running free' then so be it. I am afraid that mine tend to come back when they have either killed or lost whatever they were hunting.

INDEX

Note: general subjects which are shown in the list of contents are not included in the index. Bold figures indicate illustrations.

1. 1972; a pairs class

LAMBOURN at Croft House, Upper Lambourn

2. 1973; a pairs class

3. 1973; obstacle racing

LAMBOURN at Croft House, Upper Lambourn

4. 1974; George Smith and dogs

5. 1976; Nick Gazelee (Ring Steward), the Author and Roddy Armytage (Judges)

LAMBOURN at Seven Barrows

6. 1976; Large Smooth Dog class

7. 1979; judges James Delahooke, Mrs Angie Delahooke, Mrs 'George' Barclay, Mrs Lilah Shennan and her nephew, James Daly, MFH, with Barry Mackaness as Ring Steward

LAMBOURN at Seven Barrows

8. 1980; five of the initial eight judges, Michael Lyne, Michael Forsyth-Forrest, John Corkhill, Mrs Tarn Riley and Brandon Cadbury

9. 1981; four of the original seven judges who were still working at 4.30pm, Moses Aaron Smith, Martin Knoweldon, Mrs Flavia Cadbury and the Author

LAMBOURN at Seven Barrows

10. 1981; the large Champion and Reserve, Mrs Lloyd's *Lucy* and Major Scott's *Rollo*

11. 1981; the Supreme Champion, Mrs Lloyd's *Lucy*

LAMBOURN at Seven Barrows

12. *Lucy* at work in 1988

13. 1982; the eight judges, John Lloyd, N. B. Powell, Roy Ware, Leslie Harrison, Dame Margot Smith, The Hon Mark Palmer Bt and Dave Todd

LAMBOURN at Seven Barrows

14. 1982; N. B. Powell presents the Supreme Championship Trophy to Mick Cawley's *Queenie* while Roy Ware looks pensive

15. 1982; the bare fist fight that finally stopped the show being run at Lambourn

LAMBOURN at Seven Barrows

16. The crowd dispersing after the fight

17. 1984; the view from the stands

LAMBOURN Mk III at Newbury Racecourse

18. 1984; the judges, John Hunt, George Smith, James Daly MFH and Carl Banner

19. The Organisers, Mrs 'Bumble' Upton, Secretary, Peter Walwyn, Chairman

LAMBOURN Mk III at Newbury Racecourse

20. A distinguished visitor, Mr M.A.Bhutto, one-time Finance Minister of Pakistan and Governor of Sind Province, who hunts wild boar in Pakistan with longdogs

21. 1985; Phil Lloyd, judge, Small Reserve Champion Mr Colling-Fletcher's *Dolly*, Small Champion Mr Lumb's *Jed* and John Bromiley, judge

LAMBOURN Mk III at Newbury Racecourse

22. 1985; Tom Davies, judge, Large Reserve Champion Mrs Newbury's *Gemma*, Large Champion Mr Squires' *Miller*, Dick Finch, judge

23. 1985; Mrs Walwyn with the Reserve Supreme Champion, Mr Lumb's *Jed*

LAMBOURN Mk III at Newbury Racecourse

24. 1985; Mrs Walwyn with the Supreme Champion, Mr Squires' *Miller*, ably handled by Karen Hemes whilst his owner was busy combining

a. Penny Lowis

b. Leesa Sandys-Lumsdaine

25. Faces at Shows

c. Michael Forsyth-Forrest

d. George Smith

a. Elspeth Mackie

b. Tony Mills

26. Faces at Shows

c. Bert Gripton

d. Roy Ware

a. 'Ginger' French

b. Sue Sowerby

27. Faces at Shows

c. Phil Lloyd

d. Maurice Salkeld

a. Caroline Gentry

b. Brian Peters

28. Faces at Shows

c. Peter Ince

d. David Gaydon

a. Eddie Jones

b. Tony Diprose

29. Faces at Shows

c. Dave McKnie

d. John Bromiley

a. Janis Willingale

b. Tony Palmer

30. Faces at Shows

c. Alf Graham

d. David Hancock

a. Delyth Jones

b. Vic Gardner, whose magazine, *Shooting News*, sponsored the SNUK Championship Show at Towcester

31. Faces at Shows

c. Dave Todd

d. Lucy Clegg

32. 1981; George Smith judging

WHADDON CHASE

33. 1982; Working Groups, Peter Ince and Ginger French

34. 1982; Thomas Morgan Davies judging the Large Rough Ring with Brian Peters

WHADDON CHASE

35. 1982; Sue Busby judging the Small Lurcher Ring

36. 1982; Family Groups

WHADDON CHASE

37. 1983; David Gaydon's Working Group

38. 1986; the organiser and his assistants, Peter Tabor with Caroline Whitlock and 'Hobblette' Dimsdale

WHADDON CHASE

39. 1986; Gwyn Williams judged the Large Rough Ring

40. 1986; Mrs Kitcher judged the Large Smooth Ring . . .

WHADDON CHASE

41. . . . and the Puppies

42. 1986; Mr Kitcher judged the Small Ring

WHADDON CHASE

43. 1986; George Sowerby presents the Sue Sowerby Trophy to the Supreme Champion, Caroline Gentry's *Sally*; Mrs Gentry was one of the subscribers to the Trophy

44. 1977; the Champion, Mrs Mactaggart's *Padge*

DENHOLM

45. The Riley Family Group, *Bru*, *Gos*, *Tarn*, *Saker*, *Ti*, *Kitty* and *Padge*

LOWTHER
46. 1980; George Smith judging in the very cramped ring

HOLKHAM
47. 1980; the Author judging in the shadow of Holkham Hall

48. 1980; the Champion, George Smith's *Eve*

COTTESMORE

49. 1985; judges Dick Finch and Gwyn Williams with the Champion, Graham White's *Chizzel*

50. 1981; the Champion, Mr Cartawick's *Sandy*

HARROGATE

51. 1982; judge Maurice Salkeld's line-up

52. 1980; Roddy Armytage judging the Large Rough ring

HEYTHROP

53. 1980; David Gaydon and Dick Finch with Large Rough Dogs

54. 1980; Trish Crotty and George Smith getting wet

HEYTHROP

55. 1982; Lees Sandys-Lumsdaine and the Author judging

Peter Goulding

56. 1981 at the Rowley Mile Stands; Sue Sowerby and her brother-in-law, Stan Surzyn
sweeping the board with *Pixie* and her son *Willow*

NEWMARKET

57. 1986 at the George Lampton Playing Fields; judges Richard Lovett and John Wignall
with the Champion, Caroline Gentry's *Sally*

1983; the Reserve Champion who also won the
edience Class

BUCCLEUCH

59. 1983; the Champion

60. 1980; judge Colin Rigden with the Champion, the Author's *Hettie*

PETWORTH

61. 1984; *Hettie* retrieving

SUSSEX LONGDOGS
    62. 1986; judges Messrs Seedhouse and Kitcher with the Champion, Mr Mears' *Tosh*

HERTS WORKING TERRIER CLUB
    63. 1986; Bill Adams, MRCVS, MFH, with the Champion, Mrs Morgan's *Asti*

CLARO BEAGLES
   64. 1986; judges Messrs Mann and Burden with the Champion, Dawn Drabner's *Peggy*

WESTON PARK COUNTRY FAIR
   65. 1986; the Reserve Champion, Mrs Samuel's *Lady* and the Champion, John Bromiley's *Isaac*

ATHERSTONE
66. 1986; judges Mr Mitchell and Mrs Cadbury with the Reserve Champion, David Gaydon's *Queen*

GRAFTON
67. 1980; Champion and Reserve, Mrs Willingale's *Pepsi* and Mr Hill's *Gypsy*

PUCKERIDGE   68. 1986; the Champion, Mrs Watson's *Badger*

FINMERE   69. 1985; the Champion; Tony Palmer's *Smokey*

FERNIE

      70. 1985; judge, Mick White with the Champion, Miss Harris' *Chcal* and Reserve, Caroline Gentry's *Sally*

PETERBOROUGH

      71. 1986; judges Messrs Burrell and Holland with the Champion, John Bromiley's *Isaac* and Reserve, Mick Gentry's *Jcnny*

72. 1978; spectators at the Kennels

OAKLEY

73. 1984 at Newton Blossomville; Sue Sowerby and Mick Gentry blasted by the wind

1987; the Sue Sowerby Trophy winner Mr Lane's *Zac*.

OAKLEY

75. 1989, at the Point to Point course; the Sue Sowerby Trophy winner, Mrs Walch's *Amy*

76. 1985; Brian Pether judging

SHOOTING NEWS U.K. Finals at TOWCESTER RACECOURSE

77. Nick Scutt judging

78. The Reserve Champion, Mr Vigor's *Joc*

SHOOTING NEWS U.K. Finals at TOWCESTER RACECOURSE

79. The Champion, Caroline Gentry's *Sally*

80. *Tarn*

DOGS I HAVE LIKED (where a dog's name is not known the place and date are given)

81. *Rummage*

82. *Hettie*

DOGS I HAVE LIKED

83. *Fagin;* these three were litter sisters and brother, out of *Tarn*

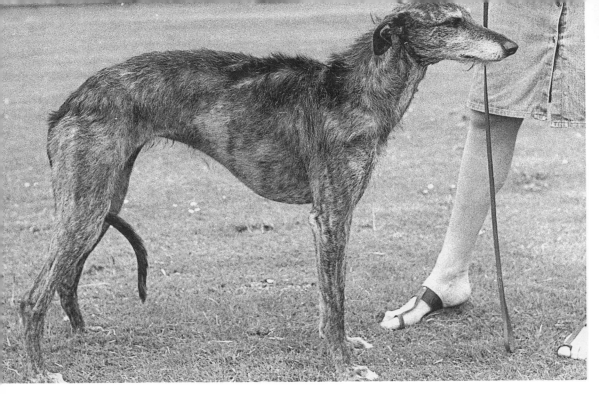

84. *Solo*, 1985

DOGS I HAVE LIKED

85. *Ryc*, 1977

86. *Bruce*, 1984

DOGS I HAVE LIKED

87. *Solo*, 1985

88. *Barncy, 1982*

DOGS I HAVE LIKED

89. *Gypsy, 1978*

90. Glynclydach, 1984

DOGS I HAVE LIKED

91. *Kauli*, 1982

92. *Tip*, 1986

DOGS I HAVE LIKED

93. *Gyp*, 1986

94. *Amy*, 1987

DOGS I HAVE LIKED

95. *Shady*, 1989

96. *Fleet*, 1989

DOGS I HAVE LIKED

97. *Pepsi*, 1983

98. *Biff*, 1976

DOGS I HAVE LIKED

99. *Peggy*, 1986

100. *Fly*, 1983

101. *Monk*, 1989

102. *Tcss*, 1987

DOGS I HAVE LIKED

103. *Shoshi*, 1988

104. *Alice*, 1985

DOGS I HAVE LIKED

105. Hallaton, 1986

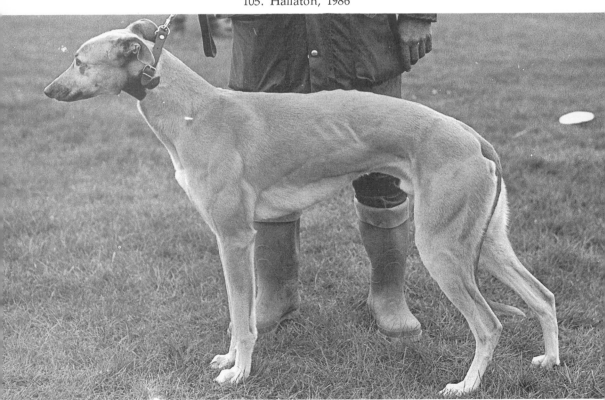

106. Worcester, 1988

DOGS I HAVE LIKED

107. *Gyp*, 1985

108. A laid-back shoulder in order to stretch out forwards

REQUIREMENTS OF THE LONG DOG

109. Hind legs brought well forward under the body

110. Power and extension behind

REQUIREMENTS OF THE LONG DOG

111. Strong legs and feet to stand the strain of turning at up to 35mph

112. *Sally* stretched out, unbalanced, with her head held up

SHOWING A LURCHER

113. *Sally* standing naturally

114. To watch dogs moving imagine a fence or wall with a gap and watch each dog individually as it crosses this gap. Unless the class is very small at least six circuits will be needed to see them all properly

JUDGING LURCHERS (the Author judging)

115. Then go to a corner and watch them all coming towards you; turn round and watch them going away

116. Look at the front, head and teeth

JUDGING LURCHERS (the Author judging)

117. Run a hand down the neck and along the back; check the number of knuckles between the shoulder blades and between the hip bones

118. Look at the dog from the front, side and rear

JUDGING LURCHERS (the Author judging)

119. Send the dog out, across and back to see again how it moves

120. Face, eyes and teeth

GEORGE SMITH judging at Lambourn/Newbury

121. The chest muscles are a good guide to a dog's fitness

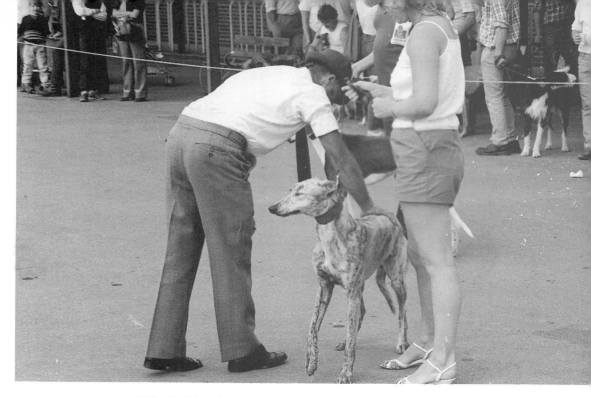

122. Pushing down on the quarters to check the leg muscles

GEORGE SMITH judging at Lambourn/Newbury

123. Sending them round again before bringing in the ones he wants

124. Holkham, 1980, with seven pipe bands practising within ear-splitting distance of the lurcher ring

THE UNUSUAL

125. Petworth 1985 drenched; Mick Cawley who gallantly judged all day in monsoon-like rain with the Champion, Donald Ralph's *Tess*

126. Glynclydach 1987; *Quis judicavit ipsos judices?*: Thomas Morgan Davies caught bending

THE UNUSUAL

127. Sartorial elegance rarely seen at lurcher shows; Michael Clayton, Editor of *Horse and Hound*, judging at the Oakley

128. Lambourn, 1972; it was a horseshoe course with a fairly sharp bend

OTHER SHOW ACTIVITIES   RACING

129. Lambourn, 1977; note the difference in the crowd and car park

130. Newmarket 1986; Gary Kelly slips two greyhounds for the Cup

RACING

131. Newmarket 1987; two lurchers stride for stride

132. Sussex Longdogs; showing how necessary it is to use muzzles. Watch the brindle in the centre

RACING

133. The brindle dog has come across the white to fight the nearer brindle

134. The white recovers himself

RACING

135. Without muzzles a fight would now be on

136. North Bucks Show, 1979. At right rear is the chute leading to the handler who let dogs go when the owner started to call or whistle from the far end

SPEED JUMPING

137. The same; Mark Holland on the platform calls his dog whilst Sue Sowerby does the writing and the Author holds the stop watch

138. Oakley 1985; some go over . . .

SPEED JUMPING

139. . . . and some go under

140. Newbury 1985; trying hard

HIGH JUMPING

141. the same; Graham Chapple's *Lucy* wins at 8 foot 6 inches

142. Worcester 1988; Denis Eastwood sends *Radar* up . . .

HIGH JUMPING

143. . . . and over

144. Holkham 1980; Nick Jenkins with *Kanga*

SHOW JUMPING

145. Slough 1983; Sue Sowerby's *Willow*

146. Newbury; 'Stay there!'

OBEDIENCE

147. but not for long

148. N.L.R.C. Field Trials; steady to ferret

OBEDIENCE

149. The same; going for the bolting rabbit without permission

150. The Squire goes a'coursing; the spaniels helped to push hares up

PRIVATE COURSING AS IT WAS

151. Lord Rivers looks for a hare

152. There two licensed officials. The Judge, who is mounted; Bob Burdon at Huntingdon

PUBLIC COURSING TODAY

153. and the Slipper who is on foot; Gary Kelly at Huntingdon

154. Rule 18; taking dogs to slips. The handlers bring two dogs to the Slipper who is standing in the shy. In the background are others waiting their turn to run

SOME RULES OF THE NATIONAL COURSING CLUB

155. Rule 18 (4); each dog wears a coloured collar, red on the left and white on the right (*Canterbury Pink* and *Genette*)

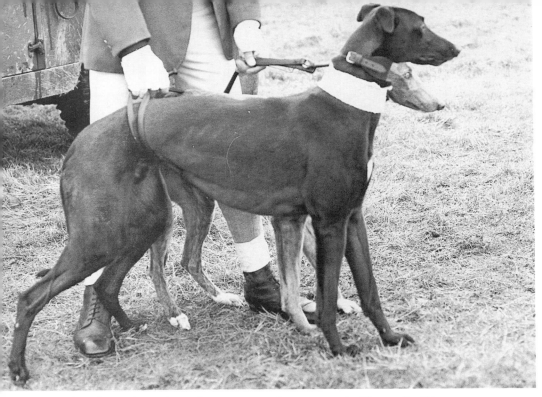

156. Two fit 80lb greyhounds ready to run can take some controlling so the Slipper wraps the slack of the slip lead round them to hold them together (*Silvery Moon* and *Sir Mick*)

157. Rule 19 (2); handlers may go forward up the running ground to catch their dogs at the end of the course

158. The 'shy' behind which the Slipper stands can be a screen or a pile of straw bales, (Bob Blatch at Newmarket)

SOME RULES OF THE NATIONAL COURSING CLUB

159. or it can be a vehicle of some sort (Gary Kelly with *Ballinvella* and *Millrace Joe*)

160. Rule 20, 'The Slip shall be made at the sole discretion of the Slipper . . .'

SOME RULES OF THE NATIONAL COURSING CLUB

161. 'The length of slip . . . should not be less than 80 yards'

162. The Slipper makes sure that the dogs have seen the hare

SOME RULES OF THE NATIONAL COURSING CLUB

163. By the time that the hare reaches the slipping distance the Slipper should be running forward

164. Rule 20 (1); The Slipper has to be certain that the hare is not lame or 'balled up' with mud

SOME RULES OF THE NATIONAL COURSING CLUB

165 On their way

166. Rule 20 (4); once the dogs are slipped they shall not be touched . . . until the Judge has given his decision . . .'

SOME RULES OF THE NATIONAL COURSING CLUB

167. Rule 21; ' . . . it shall be the duty of any person . . . who is in the vicinity of any hare brought down . . . to satisfy himself that the hare is dead . . .'

168. Rule 22 (2); ' The Judge shall, on the terminat[ion]
of each course, immediately deliver his decision . . .
displaying a red or white handkerchief corresponding [to]
the collar of the winner . . .' (Ronnie Mills at Cotswol[d]

SOME RULES OF THE NATIONAL COURSING CLUB

169. Rule 22 (3); 'He shall not not recall or reverse his
decision on any pretext whatsoever . . .'

170. The Judge is mounted so that he – or she – can ride as near as possible at right-angles to the line of the hare and dogs (Walter Dick at Newmarket)

SOME RULES OF THE NATIONAL COURSING CLUB

171. The Judge must be ready for the unexpected (Sheena Boutflower at Cotswold)

172. Rule 23; ' . . . the dog which scores the greatest number of points during . . . the course is to be declared the winner'

SOME RULES OF THE NATIONAL COURSING CLUB

173. ' . . . estimating the the value of the work done by each dog, as seen by the Judge, . . .' (Bob Burdon at Huntingdon)

174. Speed to the hare; a one length lead for one point for white collar

SOME RULES OF THE NATIONAL COURSING CLUB

175. A two length lead for two points for white collar

176. A four length lead for three points for white collar

SOME RULES OF THE NATIONAL COURSING CLUB

177. A five lengths lead for three points for red collar and one point for the kill

178 (a, b and c). The Turn is where the hare is brought round at not less than a right-angle from her previous line

179. The Wrench is where the hare is bent from her line at less than a right-angle

SOME RULES OF THE NATIONAL COURSING CLUB

180. The difference between a Turn and a Wrench is a matter of degrees

181. The Kill, '. . . not more than one point . . . but may be of no value'

SOME RULES OF THE NATIONAL COURSING CLUB

182. The Trip, or unsuccessful attempt to kill. This hare picked itself up and escaped under a wire fence beside the photographer

183. Rule 25; '. . . no dog shall receive any allowance for a fall'

SOME RULES OF THE NATIONAL COURSING CLUB

184. Rule 27; 'If a second hare be started . . . '. Red collar, on the right, is coursing the original hare while white collar has seen a second hare and has started off after it

185. Rule 28; 'Any person allowing a dog to get loose . . . shall be fined . . .'

SOME RULES OF THE NATIONAL COURSING CLUB

186. The course is not necessarily ended when a third dog joins in

187. Rule 30; for a 'No course' the Judge waves his arm

SOME RULES OF THE NATIONAL COURSING CLUB

188. For an 'Undecided' the Judge takes off his hat

189. Netting hares on an estate (where a hare shoot was about to take place) for removal to another estate where there was a hare shortage

NETTING HARES

190. Lifting a hare from the net; this is a highly skilled job and hares must be held in a particular manner to avoid stress

191. The special boxes in which hares travel

NETTING HARES

192. Loading boxes onto the waiting Land Rover

193. The greyhound is a sprinter rather than a stayer

COURSING: THE PURE BREEDS   GREYHOUNDS

194. Exercising greyhounds in the days before motor vehicles made roads unsafe

195. At a coursing meeting the running ground is usually walked to clear it of hares; (Slipper Brian Pether at Cotswold)

GREYHOUNDS

196. Clearing the ground (Slipper Roger Upton at Cotswold)

197. Huntingdon, the Judge and dogs (*Lollipop* and *Flower Drum*)

GREYHOUNDS

198. *Timworth Billy* and *Always First*

199. *Ballahulish*

GREYHOUNDS

200. *Juniper* and *Widget Mink*

201. *Royal Mardi Gras* and *Baddanloch*

GREYHOUNDS

202. *Royal Mardi Gras* and *Baddanloch*

203. *Get Happy*

GREYHOUNDS

204. Two puppies run wide

205. *Buckshee*

GREYHOUNDS

206. Two tired dogs, *Really Erica* and *Widget Minniver*

207. John Hamilton with *Summer Choir* and *No Trump*

WHIPPETS

208. John Cooper runs for the hare with *Ch. Withaway Nimrodel* and *Silver Moppet*

209. Almost all whippet coursing meetings are walked; a long line out on short grass.

WHIPPETS

210. A short line on thick stubble to ensure that hares are not walked over

211. The Slipper (Bob Blatch) walks 20 yards in front of the line with the two dogs to run

WHIPPETS

212. Two whippets on stubble; the length of slip is necessarily shorter than that for greyhounds

213. *Summer Choir* and *Nia of Nipalong*

WHIPPETS

214. *Summersway Echo;* note the relative size of whippet and hare compared to that of greyhound and hare

215. *Martinsell Seaweed* and *Moondyne Snipe*

WHIPPETS

216. Whippets have stamina as well as speed; *Ch. Withaway Nimrodel* and *Tamalinden Tilia*

217. Two under-18-inch whippets are slipped . . .

WHIPPETS

218. . . . and come back carrying the hare between them while the Judge gives the white flag for *Nimrodcl Djakarta*

R. Jeffries

219. A saluki meeting at Shipton Court in 1927. Mr W. C. Jeffries, Miss May Jeffries and the Judge Mr Skinner. Note the double slips

SALUKIS

220. As for whippets, most saluki meetings are walked

221. Salukis can be held in single or double slips according to the owner's wishes

SALUKIS

222. A hare gets up in stubble and the spectators try and join in

223. Salukis are stayers, not sprinters; *High Stakes* and *Xerxes*

SALUKIS

224. *Xerxes* and *Joshuas Annie*

225. *Xquisite* and *High Life*

SALUKIS

226. *Xquisite* and *High Life*

227. Deerhounds were not originally bred for coursing hares but many take to it well

DEERHOUNDS

228. Most deerhound meetings are walked

229. Lurchers, whippets and a borzoi in Northamptonshire

COURSING WITH LURCHERS

230. Lurchers only, in Lincolnshire

231. The meeting can be formal, with a Slipper and a Judge (on foot)

COURSING WITH LURCHERS

232. Lurchers are usually held in single slips

233. Walking up a hare

COURSING WITH LURCHERS

234. Slipping on rape

235. A less formal meeting will dispense with the slipper and owners will slip their own dogs, the two to run walking in front of the line

COURSING WITH LURCHERS

236. At an even less formal meeting where dogs are slipped from where they walk the line can be half a mile long

237. The line needs to be shorter on cover, such as rape, or hares will be walked over

COURSING WITH LURCHERS

238. Lurchers are not as fast as greyhounds but from their cross-breeding can have tremendous stamina

239. A fawn and a brindle turn the hare from a wood

COURSING WITH LURCHERS

240. A hare off rape making for the wood and safety

241. Lurchers coursing

COURSING WITH LURCHERS

242. Lurchers coursing

243. A solo course

COURSING WITH LURCHERS

244. This hare beat the two dogs by spinning round on its hind legs every time they snatched at it until it got to the wood in safety

245. Two rough dogs settle down for a long run

COURSING WITH LURCHERS

246. As in public coursing, a third dog does sometimes join in

247. *Len* carrying the hare

COURSING WITH LURCHERS

248. *Badger* very tired